THE RESILIENT ACTOR

THE RESILIENT ACTOR

HOW TO KICK ASS IN THE BUSINESS (WITHOUT IT KICKING YOUR ASS)

DEBRA WANGER

LIONCREST
PUBLISHING

THE RESILIENT ACTOR

How to Kick Ass in the Business (Without It Kicking Your Ass)

ISBN   978-1-61961-830-5 *Paperback*

        978-1-61961-831-2 *Ebook*

This book is for the unhealthy, out-of-balance girl I used to be. She learned a lot of hard lessons on her path to becoming a balanced, resilient actor.

May her lessons light a path for you.

CONTENTS

FLASHBACK

What happened to my life?

I was living my dream as an actor in the theater—a dream I'd fantasized about for years.

In my dream, I was smiling and happy, healthy and loved. This life—my theater life—wasn't a dream at all.

Being on stage was wonderful. I could play happy. I could play healthy. I could sing my heart out, lost in the moment on stage. The cast was like a family to me and I felt connected to the people in the audience.

But off stage, my life was depressing. I went home every night to my sad reality of loneliness and solitude. I wasn't happy or healthy. Most nights I binged on cake and TV.

I'd stay in bed until noon. Curled up under the covers with the shades drawn, I thought about giving up. Who did I think I was? I was a sham. My skin was breaking out and I was overweight. I was always tired, but no matter how much I slept, energy eluded me. No matter how much I ate I still felt empty inside. I'd drag myself out of bed, flop onto the couch, and watch soap operas. Then I'd head to the theater, clean up, make up, and dress up for another brave performance. Brave—ha! I was a disaster.

On the outside, I appeared happy and healthy-ish, but on the inside, I was falling deeper and deeper into a black hole. I wanted to (and did) stop acting for a while, but instead of abandoning my dream, I crawled out of that hole. I took back my dream and learned how to survive and thrive in the theater.

This is the book I wish someone had handed me decades ago when I began my acting career. It would have saved me years of misery. I can't go back in time to help that lost, lonely girl, so my goal is to help future actors avoid the mistakes I made on my path to health and happiness as an actor.

In the following pages, I'll let you in on the secrets I've uncovered since those early days—tips, tricks, and hacks that made me the sane, resilient actor I am (or at least, try to be) today.

Toni Morrison said, "If there is a book that you want to read, but it hasn't been written yet, you must be the one to write it."

So I did.

Let me tell you how my world fell apart, and how I put it back together.

BACKSTORY: FROM DREAM TO NIGHTMARE

I started acting at nine years old and kept performing every chance I got. Acting classes, children's theater, community theater, and choir—I did it all through elementary and junior high school. Without theater, high school in Chicago would've been a total wash, but acting gave me a place to belong. I knew immediately that performing on stage was what I wanted to do—it just took many years for me to figure out how to do it without losing myself in the process. Back then, there were no guidebooks, blogs, or online videos to teach aspiring actors how to keep balance in their lives.

At seventeen, I moved to Ohio to attend the University of Cincinnati's College Conservatory of Music, one of the best and most competitive musical theater programs in the country. I was one of only twenty-four students accepted into the program. We had to re-audition every semester, and if you failed the "boards" two semesters in a row you were asked to leave.

A lovely man (who I'm still friends with) ran the program during my first year. He was nurturing and kind, and studying theater with him was inspiring. I was doing what I loved in a great program, surrounded by vibrant, passionate people. Everyone was at the top of their game, and I was so young, taking it all in.

However, that atmosphere changed my sophomore year when a new guy was brought in to run the program. He had a different style of teaching and an attitude often found in the theater world, one that favored the patriarchy and expected you to conform to the system. Many instructors believe the way to build you up as a performer is to first break you down. They believe it makes you more flexible and resilient. That militaristic style of instruction is like boot camp: you aren't allowed to have an identity or a personality, and you certainly aren't allowed to have an opinion. They torture you. The new instructor spoke with a gentle South African accent. Although the tone of his voice sounded warm, the words he spoke were sharp, cunning, and, at times, very cold. He'd say things to me like, "If you don't lose weight, you'll never work in this business." He said other things like... well, I'd need a couple of shots of whiskey to repeat them.

Maybe he thought he was toughening us up for the rejection we'd face auditioning for parts in New York. Many students at the conservatory had been stars in their hometowns and probably needed some toughening, but I was used to rejection. I had to fight for leads in high school, and while I got some of them and did quite well, I didn't get them all. Being rejected for a role hurt, but those early experiences prepared me for the rejection that comes with a professional acting career. I didn't need to be toughened up or beaten down, and I didn't have the maturity, stability, or the "edge" to have someone jack with me like that.

I felt out of balance in so many ways. My emotional health was out of whack and that instructor crushed any shred of self-confidence I had mustered by that age. All the unresolved issues from my childhood had left me pretty raw. I could have experimented with drugs, sex, and alcohol, but instead turned to emotional eating.

Around this same time, someone attempted to break into my home. They repeatedly body slammed my front door, trying to get into my apartment while I was sleeping there alone. This scared the pants off me. I was already very tender from the mind games at school, and this close call was more than I could bear.

One thing was certain in my mind: if I stayed at the Conservatory, I'd never achieve the balance I needed. The healthiest part of me knew that I had to get out of there.

That's when an opportunity fell into my lap. I was offered a part in a Florida production of *Fiddler on the Roof*. It was February in Cincinnati, which made a few months in Florida even more enticing. *A geographical cure*. Maybe I could take some time off from school to do the show and then decide whether I wanted to come back to the Conservatory.

I wrestled with that decision because, if you get through the musical theater program at the Conservatory, it's like graduating from Harvard Business School. You get a golden ticket that opens doors in New York. Many of my hardworking friends from the Conservatory have successful, lucrative acting careers, performing on Broadway and around the world.

I was eighteen, and had convinced myself that accepting that role was another step in my acting career. Deep down, I hoped it was the change I needed. It took me a while to get over the regret of dropping out of school, but now I think if I'd stayed in the program, I would have crashed and burned earlier and worse than I eventually did.

After *Fiddler on the Roof* ended, I kept working in the theatre, got my Equity Card, and stayed in Florida for four more years. During that time, the theater was everything to me. As long as I was in a show, I had a sense of belonging and purpose, and a built-in social life with the cast.

When you're working, you spend a lot of time with your cast. You rehearse with them and do eight shows a week together, sometimes more. When you act, you interact closely with them. Sometimes you pretend to be their parents or their children, or you have to pretend you're in love with them. You perform together, hang out together, and party together. If you go on tour, you may room together and the only people you know in the city is your cast.

I had limited life and social skills, but as long as I was working, I felt that I was on track. But between shows, I felt like I had no value. I needed someone—a director, a cast, an audience—to tell me I was good enough. Lost, lonely, and depressed, my eating and sleeping habits were horrible and there was no one to talk with about it. I tried to fix the loneliness in my life and ended up in unhealthy relationships. My life was totally out of balance because my self-worth depended on being in a show.

I tried therapy. While working with me on my abandonment issues, my therapist got engaged and suddenly moved to Turkey. She was the first of two therapists I had who moved to foreign countries mid-therapy. I appreciate the irony now, but at the time, it didn't help me.

I tried a string of diets and natural health cures in a half-baked attempt to save myself. Of course, I had no idea what I was doing, but it started me on a path to what would eventually lead me to some answers. I was overweight and bingeing, so I tried purging, but (and I'm grateful for this now) I wasn't a good vomiter. I tried fad diets and none of them worked, so I spent my days eating in front of the television. I was doing the best I could with all the bad information I was given by the diet industry, and I failed at all of it.

Acting had been the high that pulled me out of my lows and saved me from my depression and loneliness, but somewhere along the way, even that had stopped working. I was young and talented, but I saw myself as horrendously fat and worthless. I had bad acne flare-ups caused by stress and compounded by my poor diet, and that added to my insecurity. And romantic relationships, intimacy issues, letting people know the authentic me...add those to the whiskey shot conversation agenda.

I thought, *Is this all there is? Is this my life?*

I had left the Conservatory thinking a professional career would save me, and I realized that acting, singing, and the theater had become my everything—and they weren't enough. That realization was devastating. If my life wasn't about acting, what was it about? Who was I, if not an actor? Something had to change. I needed balance. I needed purpose. I was sinking fast and if I didn't do something I'd never bounce back.

Up until that point in my life, I believed acting was the only thing of value that I had to give to the world. Now I knew that in order to achieve balance, I had to ditch acting.

RECOVERY TAKE 1: BOSTON TO HOLLYWOOD

I found structure and purpose by going back to school. I moved to Boston, and enrolled in the bachelor of sociology program at Tufts University. Around the same time, I got into a 12-step program to help me with my overeating, reconcile a lot of baggage from my past, and start to let people know the real me. I discovered this "real person with a normal life" stuff wasn't so bad. I could do it!

I barely mentioned to anyone that I had been an actor in a previous incarnation, and to my surprise, they still wanted to hang out with me. They didn't know I could perform, sing high, or be someone else for a while. They liked the real me who wasn't performing, and accepted me as someone other than an actor.

Graduating magna cum laude was validating—I was intelligent and capable enough to take on other careers. I interned for the morning show on Magic 106.7 and that led to a full-time job in Boston radio. The realization that I could be successful outside the theater was a turning point for me. Feeling confident and whole, I decided to give the industry another try.

I left Boston and moved to Los Angeles to learn the business side of theater and film. At the time, superagent Michael Ovitz ran Creative Artists Agency, the biggest talent agency in the world. Ovitz changed the movie industry by shifting the focus of power from studios to agents. He's credited with single-handedly making agents the most powerful people in Hollywood.

The early '90s were the peak of agency power. His company represented some of Hollywood's biggest actors, directors, and writers. I had daily contact with movie stars and conversations with Oscar-winning actors and directors. I met everybody—people like Tom Cruise and Tom Hanks, and I completely embarrassed myself in front of Sean Penn and Shaun Cassidy. It was fun—for a while.

If I'd come to Los Angeles straight from Florida, my life would've been a disaster. My time in Boston had made me more secure and I'd lost some weight, but I still had a lot of lessons to learn. Unfortunately, most lessons are learned by falling on your face.

Hollywood agents didn't cut their assistants any slack. Being a jerk was part of the culture and felt like a rerun of my last semester at the Conservatory. Instead of a cruel instructor, I had a young, hotshot boss. He yelled a lot and threw tantrums when he didn't get his way. If a cover letter wasn't worded exactly the way he wanted it, he'd throw it at me. There was pressure for everything to be done fast and perfect and, if it wasn't, it was the assistant's fault. The normal politeness you expect in the workplace didn't exist. Some of the agents were rude and demanding, and some of the directors and executives were just as mean. "Don't you know who I am?" I heard that often. The unstated attitude was that I should be grateful to have the job, and they could replace me at any time. I've heard it said that Hollywood is like high school with money. It's true. And I hated high school.

We worked long hours and, after clients left, we assistants scurried like rats to get the leftovers from the big food spreads. I was "in the food" again, bingeing on bagels and sandwiches. I ate to fill that black hole welling up inside of me, ballooned up, and went spiraling back into depression.

RECOVERY TAKE 2: MOVIES TO TELEVISION

I was so miserable that I quit my job at the agency to get some distance from the business and figure out my next steps. I didn't want to give up my career in the industry, but I needed to find a better fit. After a short break, I went back to the agency, this time working for a television agent. It was pilot season, which had its own special kind of insanity, and got hired by a great boss—and that made a huge difference.

During pilot season, the networks scramble to make more

shows than they can bring to the air. My desk was always piled high with casting notices, breakdowns, and scripts. So much effort went into creating and casting dozens of pilots, even though we all knew most of the shows wouldn't make it on the air. The pace was manic but invigorating, and I liked the atmosphere of TV. Television people had a different attitude than film people. They worked hard but weren't so intense. They knew how to have a good time and didn't take themselves so seriously. At the time, there wasn't much crossover between movies and TV, and actors did one or the other (that divide is gone and now it's cool for movie actors to do television).

The agent I worked for had been a casting director for a long time. She didn't yell and throw things or buy into the abusive agency BS. Instead, she was fun and playful but she got her work done. She showed me that you could be kind and successful and go home after work to a normal life. You could have kids and hang out with your family and be a whole person and still have a career in the business. From her, I learned that balance was possible (or at least attemptable), but I still needed to figure out how to get there myself.

I'd learned a lot about agencies by that time and wanted to learn something new, so I went to work for a talent manager. In very simple terms, the difference between a talent agent and a talent manager is that the agent gets an actor from job to job, while a manager focuses on the big picture, guiding an actor's entire career. Managers convince agents to consider their client for jobs that fit well into the actor's long-term career goals.

The talent manager was going to take me under her wing and teach me everything she knew about the business. Instead, she threw me into the deep end with hardly any training. It was fun escorting clients to Sundance and the Golden Globes, but mostly I didn't know what the hell I was doing. She fired me in less than a year. I didn't realize it at the time, but losing that job was a gift wrapped in s**t. It was a painful experience but one of the best things that could have happened to me.

RECOVERY TAKE 3: I GOT A JOB AT THE MALL

Losing my job with the talent manager was a huge wake-up call. No one had ever fired me from anything. The film industry wasn't what I expected it to be and it lacked the creativity I craved. It wasn't at all like being in the theater. I didn't have a sense of purpose or belonging.

The gifts and the money in the movie business hide the fact that it's like any other business, just wrapped in a prettier package. I might as well have been selling cans of soup or rolls of toilet paper. Instead, I was dealing in actors. When you work in Hollywood, your lunch break is a meeting. A night out is a networking event, and you spend weekends reading scripts. It was a grind, and I didn't want to wake up in sixty years thinking, *Oops, I forgot to have a family, friends, and fun. But hey, I did read five thousand bad movie-of-the-week scripts!* The years can get away from you.

I wanted to reinvent myself again, but into what, and where? I tried to visualize what I wanted my life to look like and imagine what my ideal life could be. The funny thing was, once I put my dream life into words it didn't seem that far-fetched. It was a real, reachable goal.

In my ideal life, I lived in a house by the ocean in a beautiful town like San Diego or Santa Barbara. I had a nice Jewish boy for a husband, two kids, and a dog. I had an acting career, did some teaching, and played harp in a sunny window in my home by the sea. I'd always wanted a harp, but my parents wouldn't let me have one when I was a kid. My mother thought a harp was too big for her to haul around.

My dream life wasn't outrageous. My dream was normal, balanced, and fun.

So I left Hollywood, moved to San Diego, and got a job at the mall working for Franklin Covey, the Franklin Planner people. Working in retail was a major shift from my exciting but high-pressure agency career, but it was also a huge relief—exactly what I needed at the time.

Franklin Covey isn't just a retail store, it's a whole culture. It's based on the teachings of Benjamin Franklin (himself quite the self-improvement junkie and scheduler) and those of Stephen Covey, who wrote (among others) the book, *The Seven Habits of Highly Successful People*. I took classes on goal setting and productivity so I could teach customers how to use the products. Of all the places I could've worked, it's lucky I ended up in a place that taught me the things I needed to get my own life together. Working at Franklin Covey was an important step in getting my life situated. That experience was like a puzzle piece that gave me the skills I needed to build on all the other pieces of my life.

REDEMPTION: FROM NIGHTMARE TO DREAM

Ten years had passed since I'd been on stage, and I missed it. I was ready to go back. This time I *chose* to go back; it was a conscious decision and not an act of desperation because that's all I had—or was. I was a whole person who remembered how it felt to have a talent for a career I enjoyed.

I joined the Actors' Equity Liaison Committee, the local arm of the stage actors' union. Sitting in meetings with

Equity higher-ups, I learned about unions, producers, contracts, and negotiations. I ended up heading the local committee of that organization for about ten years.

At the same time, I wanted to get back to class to sharpen my rusty performance skills. San Diego State University offered a master of fine arts in the musical theater program. On a whim, I called the school on a Friday for information. There was one more audition for the cycle, scheduled for the following Wednesday. Fatefully, the woman running the program had been a guest director at my college in Cincinnati (small world!) and she remembered me. I scrambled to find monologues and songs, and I showed up at the audition. The school allows just ten people into the program each cycle, and I was one of them.

It felt good to reconnect with the joy of acting and to perform again. In the program, I learned to teach, direct, give lectures, and juggle all the pieces of a career in the theater. It was a small group—just ten students and the professors—and we completely geeked out on musical theater. These were "my people" and we shared the same passion for the theater! Another bonus: the school offered me a free-ride scholarship. In exchange, I taught acting to non-major undergraduates.

Collegiate musical theater was different this time around. I knew how tough it was out there and, after years in the workforce, I enjoyed my geeky grad school academic bubble. My mental state wasn't where it had been years before and the program wasn't nearly as cutthroat. Going back into acting by choice—and not because it was all I had—felt wonderful.

In the meantime, I also educated myself about exercise and nutrition. I'd been so misinformed! I got to work on myself and my skin cleared up, I lost weight, and my mind was clearer. I got (and then lost) that nice Jewish boy, I got the two kids (plus a bonus one), and I finally got my harp.

Finally, I broke into the San Diego theater community where I still perform today. I do a few shows every year and sometimes I'm offered parts without even auditioning. Although I'm happy to be a working actor, I don't depend solely on acting for my self-worth. The desperation I struggled with early in my career is gone. In its place, a newfound harmony in my life allows me to enjoy the theater. After years of being miserable, I found balance with family, friends, and career.

I also teach, and introduce middle school students to the theater. Acting had been a lifeline for me at their age, and it feels good to pay it forward. That feeling of satisfaction and fulfillment inspired me to help more people.

During this time, while I continued to search for health

and nutrition answers—no matter how unconventional—I stumbled upon the blogs of Dave Asprey. His work, which evolved into The Bulletproof Diet, was filled with nutrition advice totally contrary to most of what I'd always been taught, but it worked for me. By now, everyone has heard of Bulletproof Coffee, but I was secretly putting butter in my coffee long before anyone had ever heard of such a thing. I lost weight, lost my cravings, gained mental clarity, and my moods became more even.

At one point, I was dating a guy who had given up on losing weight. Using what I'd learned from Dave, I coached him to lose eighty pounds. He was so happy with his results, he said, "You're really good at this. You should be a professional coach." I told him that if the Bulletproof people ever offered a coaching program, I'd be the first person to sign up! Lo and behold, they did—and I did. I trained for a year with Dave Asprey and was one of the first fifty students to get certified as a Bulletproof Coach. When you get to the nutrition section of this book in Scene 4, you'll see that many of my ideas on the subject are based on what I learned through Asprey's teachings and the in-depth certification process. Now, as a health and lifestyle coach, I guide my clients on their own personal quests for health, happiness, and resilience.

I spent years figuring out how to stop pretending to be happy *and* how to stop letting this business kick my ass. I learned how to stay motivated, be productive, and maintain a healthy mindset, while meeting the primal needs for nutrition, sleep, and exercise. I cover each topic in this book to help you develop the actor's mastermind for a balanced life. I'll guide you through the same process I went through to figure out exactly what you want and make a plan to get it.

Above all, my resilience kept me going. Every time I got knocked down by a cruel instructor, an evil boss, a bad diet, a pink slip, or a nasty breakup, I got back up again. I had to reinvent myself each time, but I never gave up. You can fall into that black hole and never come out. Or you can bounce back from disappointments, challenges, and rejections. Bouncing back is a lot easier with a balanced life. This book is about cultivating that balance and becoming resilient. This career can kick your ass, or you can kick ass in it.

THE SPOTLIGHT'S ON YOU

This book is for actors who got seduced into the unhealthy acting lifestyle. It's for anyone who bought into the myth that to be a performer, you have to smoke, drink, and stay up all night. It's for actors who believe they have to be negative, mean, and miserable.

It's for young actors who haven't yet fallen into these traps, so they can avoid them.

This book is also for actors who've been unhealthy so long they've given up hope. It's never too late to feel better, look better, and have a happier life. There's always an opportunity to bounce back and turn your life around.

Finally, this book is for anyone in a creative field. Taking care of yourself will help you in any demanding career.

The wisdom I share with my private coaching clients is the same wisdom that I want to share with you in this book. I'll guide and support you on your path to having a sane and happy life in this challenging profession. I've been there and I know the way.

There are two acts in this book and you have a starring role in both of them. It's time for the performance of your life.

Act I, "Find Your Ideal Balance," starts with the end in mind— what you want your life to be. I want you to shine a big bright light on all your wishes, hopes, and dreams. Imagine them, visualize them, and put them into words. Bring them out into the light. How do they fit into your busy actor's life? There's more to being an actor than acting. We'll talk about the many pieces that bring balance to your acting career.

In *Act II, "Master the Balance,"* we'll turn on the cameras. We'll work through all the logistics of creating your ideal, balanced, resilient life.

But wait! There's more!

If you need help getting started, check out my companion guide, *The Resilient Actor's Workbook: The Kick in the Pants You Need for Kicking Ass in the Business (Without It Kicking Your Ass)*, a step-by-step guide to help you put your plan into action.

Lights, camera, action! The spotlight is on *you*.

ACT I

FIND YOUR IDEAL BALANCE

Before you begin this journey, ask yourself how you define balance.

What would your ideal, balanced life look like?

In that life, how do you spend your time?

What kind of actor are you?

Where do you work?

How often do you perform?

Who do you hang out with and what do you do when you're not working?

Once you know what your balanced life looks like, the journey to achieve it becomes much easier.

For me, staying healthy is about staying centered and finding as much balance in my life as possible. I stay centered through meditation, a healthy diet, exercise and enjoy all my vices in moderation. Finding balance can be more difficult, but it's important for me to balance family, career and my social life in order to recharge my emotional life. I look for ways to challenge my views and to find empathy for others to better myself as a person and as a performer. I find working towards being a whole person by focusing on my emotional, spiritual and social life puts me in my most healthy state. One aspect may pull more focus than the others at times, but it's all about balance and bringing myself back to center. For me, this is where good health begins.

—KRISTI HOLDEN, CHRISTINE IN THE LAS VEGAS AND WORLD
TOUR PRODUCTIONS OF *THE PHANTOM OF THE OPERA*

SCENE 1

YOU'RE MORE THAN AN ACTOR

Kicking ass in this business without letting it kick your ass is about resilience. Being a resilient actor is about seeing yourself as the whole package—more than just talent. Talent is just the beginning. Getting the rest of your life in order will give you a solid base and the reserves you need to ride the waves of an ever-changing, unstable—sometimes rocky—industry. When you're rejected at an audition or out of work for a while, those reserves help get you to that next audition.

For many years, I allowed acting to define me. But I learned I was much more than an actor, and so are you. Develop other aspects of yourself and your life, and you will increase your chances of success as an actor and as a person.

YOUR LIFE'S SCRIPTS

When theatre becomes the entirety of your life, get yourself to a hospital and rock a crack baby ASAP. It will get your life (and theatre dreams/disappointments) in perspective.

—SIOBHAN MICHAEL CREWS

It's easy for us to identify solely as actors. The profession can be all-consuming. If you can't see yourself as anyone but "actor," try this exercise to get a different view of yourself: survey your family and friends, and ask them what they like most about you. What is it about you that makes them want to hang out with you? Listen and write down their answers. When you're done, you'll have a list of why you're awesome. More than likely, a lot of it has nothing to do with acting. Being able to separate your value from acting will make you a more resilient performer.

The next time you're rejected for a part, read that list. You're still you—your amazing, awesome self. You still matter to those people who value you for much more than your performance skills.

GIVE YOURSELF PROPS

Don't read reviews or listen to critics when you're in a show. It's not worth it no matter what they say, positive or negative. Have a life outside of theatre that will keep you balanced. Learn new skills and try new activities in life other than the-

atre. Don't become obsessed with social media. It's a rabbit hole that will never fulfill your soul. Most importantly, be satisfied with who and where you are in life. No matter how talented you are no one wants to work with someone that is angry and unhappy all the time. Find the joy in life onstage and offstage.

—ASHLEE ESPINOSA, REGIONAL THEATRE ACTOR AND ASSOCIATE
FACULTY OF THEATRE, RIVERSIDE CITY COLLEGE

All actors are unemployed at some point, even A-listers. Theater friends may come and go with a film or show, so you need other relationships. You can prop yourself up for those times with support systems outside the people you're working with. Without people outside of your acting life, you could have no work, no friends, and nothing to fall back on between roles.

If all you have to look forward to is the next audition, rejection can swallow you whole. A whole, healthy life will make you resilient so when you're rejected for a part, you can bounce back. You can be disappointed—that's normal—but you won't lose everything in the process. You'll still have other interests, friends, and activities.

Think of yourself as a boxer. If you go into the ring worn out and the only thing you have in life is winning that match, you'll get knocked out. But if you have reserves and a life waiting for you after the bout, you'll be tougher to knock down. Even if you lose the match, you'll still have something to come home to. An actor with a healthy, full life can take a lot of punches.

Health goes beyond eating right and getting enough exercise. What's in your head and your heart affects you too. Without emotional and mental health, your physical health will suffer. You need to build a life outside the theater to make that happen. There are a lot of ups and downs in this profession. A balanced life with plenty of support systems off stage will get you through those ups and downs.

When I was at a low point in my actor life, I'd relinquished power over my health and happiness to the stage. My reliance on work for value made me seem desperate when I wasn't working. Who wants to hire an unhealthy, depressed actor who believes she has no value beyond the stage?

After I invested time in relationships outside the theater, I was happier, whether I was working or not. When you're happy, people want to be around you, and they may want to hire you.

A life outside acting gives you rich experiences and greater insight that you can bring to your roles. The more you can bring to a role, the easier it'll be to put your heart into it, and the more authentic the performance will be. If you want to be believable in a role, bring some experience to it. Your audience will respond to that authenticity, that truth. A resilient actor is a happier person off stage and a better actor on stage.

LET'S GET PHYSICAL

Resilience starts with your health. I'm going to sound like your mother here, but you need to hear this: your health is your wealth. If you have your health, you have everything. It's easy to ignore those sayings when you hear them over, and over, and OVER again. They're repeated so often for a reason—they're true!

Maintaining your health can be a challenge for anyone, and for an actor, it can be even more challenging. Acting isn't a job you do from 9 to 5 and then put away so you can go home. You work irregular hours and your free time revolves around acting. It can be an all-consuming passion. Being an actor can progress from a career to a lifestyle and even a complete identity. For an actor, it's easy to believe that acting is everything and to neglect your health.

THE MENTAL GAME

Acting is a physical profession, whether you're dancing

or reciting Shakespeare for hours or doing take after take shooting bad guys in the Wild West. It's mental, too, especially when you dip into raw places to deliver convincing dialogue. You need to show up and be present, and every performance has to be fresh and energetic. If you're running on fumes your performance will suffer.

Consider the characters we play. Some of them are bonkers, and you can't play bonkers if you're not in a good place yourself. If you play a character that goes through the ringer every night and you aren't stable, it's going to drain you. In many stories, we're hired to play a character living out the most important day of their life. Some of it's hardcore: the day someone fell in love, got married, or got murdered. It's usually a big deal, and you have to be able to take the emotional hits along with the physical ones.

Being a successful actor requires more than talent. You have to be physically, mentally, and emotionally stable.

DON'T YOU HAVE TO BE CRAZY TO BE AN ACTOR?

There are myths about people in creative fields—artists, writers, musicians, and especially actors. While these myths might be true for some people, most of us in creative fields are a lot saner, smarter, and more ambitious than we get credit for.

Myth #1: We're all crazy. We're stereotypical lunatics who live impoverished, tormented lives. We stay up all night reading scripts with a tumbler of Scotch in one hand and a cigarette in the other. Those are the good nights— the nights we're not attending wild parties and sex orgies (which are really hard to maintain on an eight-show-a-week schedule). Some talented actors are so unhinged, so unreliable or intoxicated that no one wants to work with them. But you don't have to be crazy to be creative or to be an actor (although some actors are a little unhinged). It is possible to leave the drama on the stage. Most actors are hard-working, sane people. They know being reliable often pays off more than being talented. Producers, directors, and other actors want to work with people they can count on.

Myth #2: We're shallow people. Some actors are shallow. Some directors are shallow and don't want you to think, just hit your mark and shut up.

However, the best actors and directors aren't shallow. Great actors are smart and they bring more than what's in the script to every performance. Great directors encourage actors to bring depth and texture to every performance. You can't do that if you're just reading lines. Remember that life outside of acting I talked about? Just as those life experiences bring balance to your life, they'll also make you a better actor. They will bring you varied experiences, so you can bring that knowledge to your roles. You'll be a more interesting person, not just a performer or a pretty face. But don't fret—if you don't have those experiences, you can research topics around your role. The deeper the dive you're willing to make, the more interesting you'll be to the audience. Your audience wins, your friends win, and you win.

Myth #3: We're all irresponsible, professional waiters with no success in our acting careers. Not true! Just because you have a day job, doesn't mean you don't have ambition. Waiting tables puts a roof over your head and food on the table. Some actors supplement their income with a restaurant job because the hours work for their schedule. If you're a waiter and an actor, that's fine—it's a means to an end. Depending on where you live and work, you can make a living by performing. But do be careful—living in New York is every actor's dream, but you might have to work so often and hard to afford to live there that you don't have the time or energy to go to auditions.

PREDICTABILITY IN AN UNPREDICTABLE PROFESSION

Whether you picked this career, or it picked you, you went in knowing the industry was unpredictable. You might be cast in a film, stage show, or television show that then gets canceled. You could audition for a film and be on a plane for a shoot in a foreign country the next day. Changing direction with every zig, zag, and new opportunity can be dizzying.

It's tempting to use that unpredictability as an excuse for not having a whole life. A smarter option is creating predictability in the rest of your life. Structure and routine in your schedule give you a solid platform for a balanced life. A morning meditation, daily exercise, and a weekly night out with friends give you stability. Those routines also give you something to look forward to when your career isn't flying high. Including healthy habits into your routine will nourish your body and mind.

Structure, routines, and habits serve a purpose. They can take you where you want to go in life too. Before you create that solid platform, know what you want and why you want it. You can then build a structure that gives you stability while delivering your ideal life.

WHAT'S YOUR MOTIVATION? HOW TO FIND YOUR BALANCE

What you want in life—your wishes, hopes, and dreams—drives your actions. You can be more methodical and focused in your actions if you're crystal clear about your dreams. Clarity comes with understanding the *why* behind your wants—why you want what you want.

What's your motivation? Identifying your *why* will help you choose the right goals. If you don't understand the *why* behind each goal, you could be chasing a life that will never please you.

What drives your desires? Do you want to be famous? Do you want to improve other people's lives with your work? Is there a cause you care about that you want to incorporate into your life? Or do you want to make money so you can take your family on a great vacation?

Aligning your goals with your motivations—your *whys*—makes decisions easier. Once you get to the *why*, it becomes easier to choose what you want.

IMAGINE YOUR IDEAL LIFE

Think about what you want in life and why you want it. This is your opportunity to ask your fairy godmother to get out her magic wand and give you everything you want. Dream big and don't edit yourself.

It can be tough to get started if you're not used to dreaming big, so think about this: What gets you up in the morning? I'm not talking about the alarm on your smartphone. What excites you in your career, your social relationships, and your leisure time? What do you most look forward to every day? Your goals and your plan for reaching them will include more of these things. Now think about those things you *don't* have that would make you happy. Your plan will include some of those, too.

Most people never dare to imagine what their life could be. Be brave and think big. If you don't, you may shortchange yourself out of the best possible life for you. Start with the what-ifs. Start with the what-the-hells. You can edit later, but for now, you have unlimited potential. You can have and do and be *anything!*

Are you having trouble getting the creative juices flowing? Imagine your perfect day. What does that look like? Did you get a massage? Go for a hike? Take a really hard dance class? Spend some time at the Metropolitan Opera House? Watch old movies with your lover and bake the perfect pie? Film all day with Peter Jackson? Did you meditate with Deepak Chopra? Describe your perfect day and you'll get a glimpse into what makes you happy and help you clarify what you want your life to look like.

Think about your role models and why you admire them. You may have an aunt you look up to, a teacher who impressed you, or an actress whose career you'd like to emulate. Why do you admire those people? Think about their traits, values, and what makes them special to you. Think about how you can refocus your own life to reflect those same characteristics. Think about your current values. Which are most important to you? They might be family, love, adventure, contribution, excitement, autonomy, or financial freedom. There are dozens of potential values. What are yours?

VISUALIZE IT

Visualization can help you see what your life could be. Pretend you're the director of a movie in your mind that plays out your life, and include all the senses. How does it look, smell, taste? Do you feel excitement, gratitude, freedom? As an actor, pretending is one of your skills, so use your imagination! Visualizing your life can be a powerful tool to help you make your dreams a reality.

Visualize your dream career. Are you doing stage, film, musicals, commercials, or comedy? Are you doing Shakespeare? Are you a Hollywood stuntman? Are you a series regular? Are you working a little or a lot? How many shows are you doing a week?

Where do you live? Remember, this is your dream, so you don't have to settle for "uptown" or "closer to the subway;" it can be Hollywood, New York City, Des Moines, Iowa, or even Rome. In your dream city, you're an actor, but are you also writing, producing, and directing?

Visualize your life outside acting. Think about your health:

Do you want to be lighter or more fit, have more energy or mental acuity? Consider your relationships. Do you want more family time, friends time, or more time alone? Do you want to be single or in an intimate relationship? Think about your material goals too. What do you want to own as far as a home, a car? What are your goals for a savings or retirement account? Don't worry about perfection. This is an evolving, organic plan and it's all yours, so there are no right or wrong answers.

WRITE IT

Imagine it, visualize it, and then write your ideal life. Put it on paper. You may learn a lot about yourself you didn't know before this exercise. Isn't this exciting?

Jot down everything you want your dream life to be. Think about why you want that life. Do you want to live in New York City because it makes you happy? Or do you want to live there because you're a stage actor and that's where stage actors live? Think about your reasons for wanting what you want—your *why*. The answers might surprise you. Once you define your *why*, you might want to change your *what*. For example, you can be a stage actor in other cities. Then again, maybe you want to act in film. Does living in New York make sense now? Maybe you'd rather live by the ocean or in the mountains. Does living in Seattle make sense? Brainstorm about why you want your life to look a certain way. That's the first step toward identifying your goals.

Another exercise you can do to help identify your *why* is writing your eulogy. That sounds weird, I know, but go to the end of your life and write what people are saying about you. What kind of person were you, and what did you accomplish? Did you make the most of those 70, 80, 90, 100 years? Are you satisfied with the direction you're headed in now? That will bring clarity to what matters most to you, and what you discover may surprise you.

Make a conscious effort to be aware of activities that make you feel happy and healthy. Those are clues to your subconscious *whys* and possible goals that you might want to consider. Give this exercise careful thought. Dig deep and don't limit yourself—this is your life.

PUTTING WHATS TO YOUR WHYS

Now, you should have a page or more of wishes, hopes, and dreams, and a better understanding of why you want them. It's time to set some goals.

Identify those wishes, hopes, and dreams on your list that are most important to you and circle them. Now rank them in order of importance. Your dream life should be coming into focus.

If you set *too many* goals, you'll have a tough time reaching any of them. Choose the top three to five dreams that are most important to you and will have the greatest impact on your life. The next step is to come up with goals to help you realize your ideal life. In other words, you're going to assign some SMART *whats* to your *whys*.

SMART is an acronym for Specific, Measurable, Attainable, Realistic, and Timely.

- **SPECIFIC.** The more specific a goal is, the easier it'll be to break into bite-sized chunks you can do. "I want to be a successful actor" isn't a specific goal, but "I want to get three contracts in Equity Theaters this year" is specific.
  - I want to earn $10,000 as an actor next year.
  - I want to book a national commercial.
  - I want to get an agent in L.A.
  - I want to learn five new monologues.
- **MEASURABLE.** Assign a number to each one: how many, how much, how long. That'll give you something to shoot for and you'll know when you've succeeded.
  - I want to lose ten pounds or 2 percent of my body fat in the next three months.
  - I want to save $200 by February or $2,000 by the end of the year.
- **ATTAINABLE.** Instead of saying "I'm going to lose twenty pounds next week," say "I'm going to lose ten pounds in the next two months."

- **REALISTIC.** You won't likely go from making $5,000 a year acting to $20 million a year. If you set a goal like that, I appreciate your ambition, but that isn't a realistic goal. Choose realistic goals that set you up for success.
- **TIMELY.** SMART goals are short-term goals, generally a year or less. You can also have long-term goals, but for now, let's focus on goals you can reach within a year. Your year-long goals can be a smaller piece of a larger, long-term goal.

Some people don't believe in SMART goals. They think you should focus more on how you feel than what you have or what you've done. For example, instead of looking for a boyfriend to prove we are loveable, we find a way to embrace our own lovability. I agree that happiness is an inside job. Our happiness is not purely a list of accomplishments. Some people can get obsessed with crossing goals off their list and lose sight of the emotional outcome the goal will provide for them. That's why you define your *whys* first and then align your goals to them. Achieving SMART goals aligned with your *whys* will give you the life you imagined. It's not about external goals, but about what they will give you as you're achieving them. Find a way to balance means and ends goals—goals that focus on the process and those that focus on results. Focus on how you may feel if you were to achieve it and on the achievement, itself. Ideally, we can have both. We can find the pure feeling states we desire within ourselves when seeking a goal and we can also kick ass, be productive, and get s**t done with a clearly defined finish line.

Break your goals up into mini-goals and you'll have mini-successes along the way to reaching the big goal. If your goal is to get three contracts this year, your mini-goal might be to get a contract in the next four months. When you get the contract you'll be one-third of the way toward meeting your annual goal. If your goal is to lose ten pounds, you might create a plan that includes cardio training and less sugar, and then celebrate when you lose that first three pounds.

Come up with a plan that you can do and schedule it on a calendar. Consider getting an accountability buddy—a friend who's willing to join you at the gym or remind you to eat a few veggies today. Create SMART goals, schedule activities to meet them, and hold yourself accountable. You'll be more likely to achieve them.

Make them visible every day. You can use a workbook or planner or to track your goals. You can write your goals on a whiteboard, put sticky notes on your mirror, or set reminders on your phone. You can record them on your smartphone, or use a habit-tracking app. Visit my page at www.DebraWanger.com for more resources. Do whatever works for you, but do it and get it out there. Review your workbook daily so you're clear about where you're going and how to get there.

Goals give you a game plan, but you aren't enslaved to them and you don't have to drive yourself nuts with them. Your goals may evolve, or you might discover there are other ways to meet your *whys*. For example, let's say you have a goal to lose ten pounds because you want to feel healthier. If hiking three miles a day makes you feel healthy, don't worry about your weight goal—just hike every day.

As you complete a goal, cross it off your list and celebrate.

GOALS IN CONFLICT

Sometimes your goals are in conflict. I always wanted to do Stephen Sondheim's *Sunday in the Park with George*. When I was offered a part in a regional production, I was thrilled! But then I thought about how accepting the part would affect the rest of my life. I'd already committed to another show that started two days after *Sunday* ended. That gave me only two days between my last performance and first rehearsal to spend with my kids on summer break.

When your goals are in conflict, think about which of your *whys* are most important to you. That'll help you determine which goals to go after and which ones to abandon for the time being. I thought about my *why* and about my goals. Having an interesting, creative, and lucrative acting career was a top priority for me. One of my main goals was to do plays and musicals that were entertaining and stimulated thought. *Sunday* was all those things, and was in line with all my artistic goals and values. But if I agreed to do it, I'd have to sacrifice my highest value and my greatest *why*, which is my children.

That show would give me artistic satisfaction and move me closer to my career goals. But it would keep me in rehearsals all summer and that would move me away from my family goals. I imagined lying on my deathbed and asking myself, *What's the right decision?* I said no to *Sunday in the Park* and took my kids on a two-week vacation instead.

I'd be lying if I said it didn't sting to turn down that role. But I knew it was the right decision because I had so much clarity around my values and my goals. Sometimes you have to choose between goals. Figure out which of your *whys* are most important to you. Ideally, rank them in numerical order. Then the decision-making is easier and you can move on with no regrets.

If you're offered two jobs at the same time, clear, prioritized goals will make it easy for you to choose. Your acting goals might focus on money, creativity, or family. Clear goals help you make the best choices to move you closer to creating the life you imagined.

Talk with your friends about your goals. They might have some ideas for you about how they move themselves toward their goals. Just don't fall into the trap of comparing yourself to them or expecting what they do to work for you. Everyone is different and what works for one person doesn't work for everyone. Also, keep in mind that other people have different *whys* that drive them. Maybe your friends don't care so much about family, but they do care about making money. Maybe artistic satisfaction is less important to them than being in a role that gets them noticed. It's okay that everyone has different *whys*—that's what makes the world go 'round.

Values and goals are personal, and, hopefully, they represent your true, authentic self. While you may have many goals in common with other people, they have to be your own or you won't commit to them.

Review your goals and make adjustments as needed. If you're not sure they make sense, always go back to your *why*. Maria von Trapp in *The Sound of Music* always went back to the beginning, to the fundamentals. That's a very good place to start. Think about why you're doing what you're doing and ask yourself, "What's my motivation?" Your path will become clear.

OBSTACLES

Obstacles will appear and they can sabotage your goals. Think about how you'll manage them. Do you have a friend who always orders Death-by-Chocolate Brownie Cake to split with you after lunch? That'll tempt you to abandon your healthy food plan. Maybe rehearsals are starting next week and the cast is going to invite you out for drinks every evening. That'll affect your plan to cut down on alcohol, and cut into the rent money. It'll leave you hung over every morning, so you won't do your cardio workouts. Do you see how this turns into a downward spiral? Go down the what-ifs trail and figure out how you're going to overcome those obstacles. Suggest a different restaurant to your friend, skip dessert and go for a walk instead. Commit to going out for drinks after rehearsal just two nights a week and have just one drink those nights.

Most obstacles aren't surprises because you know they're going to happen. Brainstorm the potential obstacles and rehearse your responses to them ahead of time.

Be honest with yourself about your willpower. If you can't go out to lunch with your friend without eating dessert, then do something else. If you can't go to the bar after rehearsal and have just one beer, maybe going out after rehearsals won't work for you. Create a plan that works for you and is easy to follow. Keep in mind that willpower is a limited resource. The more decisions you have to make every day, the more worn down you'll get and the harder it will be to resist temptations. Later in this book, we'll discuss what you can do to make the most of your willpower, such as having a morning routine and scheduling your hardest tasks for the times of day when you have the most energy.

Anticipating obstacles will change the way you live your life. Impulsive, emotional decisions can move you away from the dream life you've imagined. Instead, you'll make thoughtful decisions that match the life you want to lead. Plan ahead. Then choose actions that bring you closer to your goals, not ones that keep you from reaching them. A plan will help you make the right decision.

AFFIRMATIONS: DOGGONE IT, PEOPLE LIKE ME!

Affirmations are the "cheese-tastic" tool of the self-help world. Remember the Stuart Smalley character from *Saturday Night Live*? Stuart told himself every day he was good enough and smart enough. That's what affirmations are: positive thoughts you say about yourself, to yourself. You can think them, or say them aloud. Your brain hears what you say—the negative and positive messages—and believes it, and we give ourselves messages all day long. Negative thoughts drag your brain down, but affirmations help you stay positive. Send your brain the right messages.

What positive beliefs do you need to achieve your goals? What negative beliefs are stopping you? How can you turn them around and make them positive affirmations?

State your affirmations in the present tense with positive words.

Instead of saying, "I will be healthy," say, "I'm healthy."

Instead of saying, "I'm not a bad actor," say, "I'm a good actor and getting better every day."

Keep in mind that your brain knows when you're BSing. If you say, "I drive a Porsche and make $100,000 a year acting," and you don't—your brain will call you on that. It knows when you're lying, so be positive, but honest too. Develop affirmations that move you closer to your goals.

Be specific in your affirmations. If your goal is to make $1 million a year acting, instead of saying "I'm going to make a million dollars a year," come up with a more specific affirmation that moves you toward your goal:

- I'm committed to auditioning at least three times a week.
- I'm committed to combing the breakdowns and going to every available audition.
- I'm committed to taking all the actions needed to become a million-dollar actor.

Affirmations are in the present tense, positive, and true.

Whenever you revise your goals, revise your affirmations. Aligned *whys* (values), goals (*whats*), and affirmations are a potent mix. You'll find it easier to keep track of your *whys*, goals, and affirmations if you write them in a workbook. When you state your affirmations, embrace the feeling, get into a strong emotional buy-in, get your whole body into it, and say it like you mean it. You can convince your brain of these new thoughts if you really act the part.

THE RESILIENT ACTOR'S WORKBOOK

The Resilient Actor's Workbook: The Kick in the Pants You Need for Kicking Ass in the Business (Without It Kicking Your Ass) is a companion guide with step-by-step instructions to help you complete the exercises in this book and put your plan into action. You'll have weekly, quarterly, and annual goals to keep you on task. Your workbook will help you track your progress and keep you motivated. You'll have easy tasks for immediate gratification, like vocal exercises or learning a monologue. Some tasks will involve adjustments to your diet and exercise routine. Lifestyle goals will improve your health and resilience. You'll look at the big picture and ask the big questions: What do I want? Why? How am I going to get there? By taking baby steps, you'll move forward each day. You'll identify, plan, and schedule your goals. Your life and career won't come together on its own—but it will with a plan, and you can make it happen.

Answering the questions in your workbook will force you to examine (or re-examine) who you are and who you want to be. Once you figure out what you want your life to look like, you can assemble the steps to get there with your workbook. It's not magic, but you can plan, schedule, execute, and maintain balance. For example, to lower your stress, you can commit to meditating for fifteen minutes a day during the next week. You'll write it down, schedule it, and do it. You can give up sugar for three days and see how you feel. You can commit to looking through the trades once a week for auditions (that's how you get work); schedule it and do it. You may have existing habits that you need to test. Maybe they're good for you and you want to keep them, but maybe they're not and you need to replace them.

Use your workbook like a portable accountability buddy to keep you on track. You can break your goals into steps that you do every week or every day. Set goals when you're ready and don't think you have to wait until the first day of the year. New Year's Resolutions don't work for a lot of us, and there might be a better time of the year for you to start.

Each chapter, or "scene," in this book ends with a "What

Can I Do Today?" section full of questions and exercises to get you started on your plan. Answer the questions and select the activities that make sense for you. Schedule them, do them, and look at the results. You're the master of your life and your acting career, and it's up to you to act.

Scene 1 got you thinking about your life's possibilities. Don't expect to have an airtight list of *whys* and wants. This is an evolving process and, as you continue through this book, you'll develop a plan.

WHAT CAN I DO TODAY?

You don't have to wait until the end of this book to begin visualizing your ideal life and planning your future. Let's start with three simple exercises to practice what you learned so far:

- Visualize what you want your life to look like. Explore every category. Where do you live? What kind of work are you doing? What are your friends like? Do you have a family? Are you in a relationship? Let your imagination go and visualize that perfect, balanced life. Don't be shy; dream HUGE—fairy-godmother style—and write it down.
- What's your biggest *why*? *Why* are you doing all this? What is the one thing in that dream life that matters to you more than anything else in the world? Your *why*

can involve your career, love life, family, finances, or anything else. Write it down.

- Think of affirmations that support your *why*. Make them present tense, positive, and true. Write a bunch of them and pick your favorite. Put it on a sticky note on your bathroom mirror. Put another one on your car dashboard. Stick one on your computer. Write it on a piece of paper and stick it in this book. Remind yourself every day of who you are—a positive person building your dream life.

SCENE 2

AUDITIONING IS YOUR JOB

Be a reader for casting directors. The single greatest way to improve your auditions is to watch others. It will blow your mind.

—DAVE THOMAS BROWN, *AMERICAN PSYCHO*, BROADWAY; *THE LEGEND OF GEORGIA MCBRIDE*, *HEATHERS*, OFF-BROADWAY; *BRIDGES OF MADISON COUNTY*, FIRST NATIONAL TOUR

At least one of your wishes, hopes, and dreams involves acting—that's why you're reading this book. You'll make progress toward your acting goals by tackling the first thing first—the audition.

People have wild misconceptions about acting. I'm often asked, "Don't you love your job? Isn't performing fun?"

Yes, of course, it's fun, but acting isn't the work—it's the perk. Rehearsing and performing takes effort, but it's also the fun part. Fun is why I got into this business and it may be why you got into acting too. But performing isn't the job—it's the bonus you get for doing the real work that's required to get hired.

The real work is finding the jobs. Looking for work and auditioning takes time, effort, and mental and emotional stamina. The sooner you commit to treating that part of your career like a job, the sooner you'll be working.

When you have a job to do, you do it even when you don't feel like it. Accountants don't think about whether or not they *feel* like balancing the books—it's their job and they do it. You have to treat auditioning the same way. Take the emotion out of it and decide it's what you need to do, whether you feel like it or not.

Schedule time every week to look for auditions. Put it on your calendar and do it whether you feel like it or not. As an actor, it's part of your job. You can check in with your agent or manager. Read breakdowns and trades, check *Backstage,* the Equity website, or ask friends where they're auditioning. "I didn't hear about it" is a lame excuse for not making it to an audition. It's part of your job to find auditions and get to them.

Lin-Manuel Miranda won't beg you to join the next tour of *Hamilton* while you're eating Häagen-Dazs in your pajamas—it doesn't work that way. Auditioning is a job and if you want to act you have to do the job—so get out there and hustle!

Go to the audition whether you think they'll like you or not. Don't let doubts mess with your head or you'll never go. The more parts you audition for, the easier it gets, and the more likely you'll get hired. Auditioning is an opportunity to get in front of directors over and over again. They may remember you and think about you when a part comes up. Go to the theater and see other actors and shows, too. As Woody Allen once said, "Eighty percent of life is showing up."

BE PREPARED, BOY SCOUT

When you have an audition, a rehearsal, or a show, you're motivated to prepare. When you have nothing planned, you shouldn't sleep all day or watch *Game of Thrones* all night. You have to treat your acting career like a job. When you're not auditioning or in a show, you still have to work. Schedule everything related to your career so you actually do it. If you leave activities like reading scripts and looking for work up to chance, you probably won't do them. If you don't do them, you won't be ready when that next audition comes around.

Similarly, if you're trying to get work in the theater, you'll be more motivated to look for auditions if you're prepared for them. Have a stack of monologues, songs, and audition material ready to go. Sometimes you may have to find a different type of monologue for a role or learn a new song for an audition, but the more material you have in your repertoire, the more likely you'll be to find auditions and go to them. As often as possible, avoid the mad rush of having to find a piece and practice it at the last minute. You'll be more excited about auditioning.

You won't always have a lot of notice or time to prepare. Be aware of shows that are coming around and have material ready in case you get to audition. If there's a tour of *Hair* coming up, have a folky rock song ready to go. If a long-running show is going to be recasting at some point, prepare for it. Somebody's always doing Shakespeare. Contemporary comedies and serious pieces are always casting, so have monologues for each type. If you're a singer, have songs for sixteen bars and one minute. Have one-minute monologues for acting auditions. Think about the type of clothing that would be a good fit for each of these auditions. Your outfits should fit well, be appropriate, and subtly reflect the character you're auditioning for.

Know yourself and your type. Be honest with yourself about the shows that are a good fit for you and focus on them, but don't limit yourself. Go to auditions that aren't a perfect fit too. You can psyche yourself out waiting for the perfect role and never go to an audition. Go, just go.

PACK YOUR BAG

An audition bag that's ready to go at a moment's notice makes it easier to go to auditions. Pack it and add a list of last-minute items, like snacks, to throw in before you walk out the door. Keep it in a convenient place at home or in your car. You aren't planning for the apocalypse, but you could end up at an audition for hours. The people may decide to go to lunch while you're waiting to audition. They may have callbacks later that day. Don't assume you'll find a healthy restaurant nearby, or a coffee machine, or even a water fountain. Bring everything you need to get through the day.

Make a checklist of these items and put it on your phone or on a note card so you can refer to it and make sure you have everything you need.

YOUR AUDITION BAG

Pack your audition bag ahead of time and keep it handy so you're not scrambling at the last minute. Adjust the items to fit where you live (consider weather, humidity, etc.) and what you need for your particular audition.

- Have your audition materials, such as sheet music and monologues. Keep them clean and organized in a binder.
- Have copies of your head shots and resume.
- Bring water.
- Bring other beverages you like to drink before and during an audition.
- Have a sweater or jacket, because you may be waiting a while in a cold room. Dress in layers so you can adjust your clothing and acclimate to the temperature.
- Depending on your city's weather, bring items like an umbrella or a rain jacket with a hood.
- Have a script to work on.
- Have a journal, notebook, or *The Resilient Actor's Workbook* to write in.
- Bring pens and a highlighter.
- Bring a charger or batteries for your cell, tablet, or other devices.
- Have a small emergency medical kit with Band-Aids, pain reliever, and any medications you're on. If you get a headache, a blister, or somehow get a paper cut in the waiting room, you'll be prepared.
- Bring healthy snacks to fill you up and help you avoid picking up junk food. Don't be hungry and miserable before your big moment.
- Bring personal items like deodorant, makeup, and a comb or brush. Also include a toothbrush, toothpaste, and breath mints, especially if you're eating. Bring eye drops, contact lens solution, and a curling iron if you need them.
- Have dance clothes and dance shoes if you're at a dance audition or if you might be asked to dance.
- Bring shampoo, soap, and a towel if you're going somewhere right after a dance audition and have a place to get cleaned up.

MAINTAIN YOUR SKILLS

You want to stay in audition-ready shape all the time. You wouldn't sign up for tomorrow's marathon and *then* start training. It's the same with auditioning. Preparing for an audition is a continuous process and you have to be consistent about it before you show up. Preparation is part of the job, and it'll take the stress out of auditioning and make you a better actor.

Always be working on your technical skills as part of your preparation for auditioning. It's easy to keep your vocal skills up when you're in a show, but what if you have months of unemployment? Do vocal warm-ups and diction exercises often. I like to record my voice lessons on my phone and then I use the vocal warm-up sections for practice. They're custom made for me because I prepared them with my voice teacher. If you don't take voice lessons, find vocal or diction exercise books and online resources to help you. You can also hire a voice coach for a few lessons and put together a vocal routine to record and practice. Stay in class—scene study, acting for the camera—whatever it takes to keep your chops up.

Working with a coach not only allows the actor to play with actions and choices, but gives the actor the confidence of the preparation which always produces a better result.

—ALLISON SPRATT PEARCE, *CURTAINS*, *CRY BABY*, *GOOD VIBRATIONS*, BROADWAY; WWW.ALLISONSPRATTPEARCE.COM

BE A PRO

Prepare for auditions as if you're going to a professional job interview. Take care of your appearance and keep your hair cut and colored to match your headshots. Have your headshots, an appropriate outfit, and the right materials prepared ahead of time. Professionalism is paramount in acting, so be on time for everything (on time is late, early is on time, remember?). If you can't be somewhere, cancel. Being late is bad, but no-showing is horrible.

If you *are* late, stressed out, or tempted to snap at someone—don't. Take a moment, take a breath, smile, and be grateful that you have the audition. It's better to be nice, even if you have nothing to gain from it; it's the right thing to do. Nobody wants to work with an inconsiderate jerk.

Remember, your audition doesn't start when you open your mouth; it starts the minute you walk into the room. It can start in the waiting room or in line. You never know who's watching. You never know who you might work with someday. Treat every human contact as a genuine relationship. These are your potential friends and coworkers. The waiting room can be a powerful place, full of opportunity. You'll miss it all if you don't show up or don't connect with people who can become your allies—or who could keep you from booking the job.

Once you have the job, continue to be one hundred percent

professional *every day*. That means being on time and knowing your lines. Have a sense of humor, but don't goof around too much, because people risked time and money on you. You have the job, but people are still watching, and they take notice of how you behave in rehearsal.

Auditions are the perfect time for insecurities and nerves to creep in. That dark part of your ego wants to mess with your head. It'll tell you you're horrible and everybody else is better for this show. Why did you even bother to show up? Expect those dark thoughts to appear in the waiting room, and prepare to knock them out. Use positive affirmations about who you are: talented, beautiful, and perfect for this show. In Act II, Scene 6, "Manage Your Mindset," I'll give you more tips for settling those jangled nerves so you can sail through every audition with confidence.

CHIN UP!

Auditioning is more fun with the right attitude. You're probably going to see people you know and that will be comforting. You'll have a chance to perform and that will make your heart sing. You may get hired—and that will be fantastic! Talk to people in line or in the waiting area and be kind, curious, and interested. Ask questions, make eye contact, and listen to the answers. They're like you and you might share similar interests. You might make a friend, or get a lead on another audition. I auditioned for a show once and met someone in line who told me about an unannounced, private audition. I got a part in that show, which ended up being a life-changing experience for me. And I dated that guy for a year! But it never would've happened if I had stood in line with my earbuds on, staring at my phone, or with my nose stuck in a book. Part of the job of acting is networking—building a community of people who can help you out, and who you can help out.

AFTER THE AUDITION

I love my craft and can't see my life without it, but the industry is a business and like all businesses is always in a state of flux.

I've found that those who are best able to navigate the currents are those who remain detached to a specific outcome. They audition for their careers and not the job. They are the ones who have full and flourishing lives outside of the industry. They are the ones that give back.

—ACTOR AND PRODUCER JEANINE ORCI, *BASEKETBALL*,
THE CURSE OF LIZZIE BORDEN 2: PROM NIGHT, AND
AUSTIN POWERS: THE SPY WHO SHAGGED ME

After you audition, follow the advice of Queen Elsa in *Frozen* and "let it go." Put it out of your mind and don't obsess about the outcome. That's easier said than done, but you did your best and nothing you can do now is going to affect the results. Journal how you felt about the audition and the feedback you got. Use that information to improve for the next one. Maybe your voice wasn't strong enough, or you fumbled your lines, or nerves or negative self-talk got the best of you. Now you know what to work on. Then start looking for the next audition. This is the *job* part of the acting job and you have to show up for that part on a regular basis.

Despite everything you do right, you're not going to book all of your auditions and you will face rejection—everyone does. You'll hear no more often than yes, and that's part of the job. Can you imagine if every actor landed every role they auditioned for? Everyone would be an actor and none of it would be special.

There's value in auditions, even if you don't get hired. They're practice and they'll make you a better actor.

YOU WON'T GET EVERY PART

This industry is extremely difficult because you are constantly being judged on everything from your talent to your looks to your resume and who you know. You are constantly being told "no" more than "yes" and you must find a way to understand and accept that a "no" does not mean you are not qualified for that job. You must turn auditions into free lessons and classes and not even expect to get the job. When you walk in the room, live in that moment only, and then leave without any expectations; then you will not rely on a "yes" as validation that you succeeded. Don't get me wrong, getting hired is the best outcome and what we all want, but you must be happy with yourself and know that you did the best you possibly could in that room or on that stage for a performance. Forget what everyone else says and follow your instincts.

—ASHLEE ESPINOSA, REGIONAL THEATRE ACTOR AND ASSOCIATE FACULTY OF THEATRE, RIVERSIDE CITY COLLEGE

Sometimes you won't get a part, usually because of something that's out of your control, like your height, your age, or chemistry. Oftentimes, you'll never know why you didn't get a job. The decision to not cast you may have nothing to do with you anyway. The fact is, oftentimes casting directors don't even know why they cast one actor instead of another. Sometimes it's a tangible reason but sometimes it's just a gut feeling. Casting is an art, and like your creative process, it doesn't always follow logic. Maybe you look too much like the casting director's ex-wife. Sometimes you're just not right for the role.

You can feel disappointed and angry, just don't get stuck there. Scream and holler, vent to your best friend, make a voodoo doll of the director, work it out, and then move on. How you handle rejection determines how quickly you bounce back for the next audition. Feel the feelings and move on. Resilience, remember? Approach every audition with a feeling of gratitude for the opportunity. Be happy for whoever gets the part, even if it isn't you. Trust that there's enough work for everybody and that you'll have your turn.

The more you audition, the less precious each one will be because every audition is a career-building step towards getting hired. Build resilience with every audition. When you show up just once a week, it hurts more to hear no. When you audition five times a week, you aren't surprised at all to get turned down and it's less of a big deal. You build a tolerance and an immunity to hearing no.

As you become more balanced in your life, rejections won't have such a devastating effect on you. I've heard no often, but over time it became less frequent. It stung less because I wasn't as invested in getting every part. As I became more resilient, I recovered faster and moved on. I know that I won't get every part and I'm okay with that. I have other interests, family and friends to fall back on. So you didn't get the part—so what? A better part will come along that you wouldn't be able to audition for if you'd gotten that role. Things have a funny way of working out.

Be kind to yourself. This is a business where you will be rejected more often than not, and 99.9 percent of the time, it has absolutely nothing to do with you. Don't beat yourself up for not being what you think they're looking for. Be prepared, show up and do your best work every time. That's all the control you have. Your time will come. In the meantime, I repeat: be kind to yourself.

—ALLEN KENDALL, *AMAZING GRACE*, BROADWAY;
PHANTOM OF THE OPERA, *ANNIE*, NATIONAL TOURS

I've survived periods of unemployment and each time I'm reminded that unemployment isn't forever. If it's your first winter, it may seem like spring is never going to get here. After you've been through a few winters, you realize that spring always arrives. The flowers will bloom again.

GET OUT OF YOUR OWN WAY

It's easy to talk yourself out of an audition. Breakdowns can be vague and tend to describe stereotypical clichéd characters. We read them and try to see where we fit by age, gender, and vocal range. Sometimes we overthink the characters and miss out on opportunities. I've talked myself out of many auditions. I'd find a casting notice, see a role that might be right for me, and come up with reasons to avoid the audition, thinking, *They'll cast someone taller, shorter, younger, or the person they usually hire is [whatever].*

I had a million excuses for not believing I'd get the part, a million reasons to skip the audition and cheat myself out of roles. I remember one audition that I was perfect for, but since they listed in the breakdown a Latina woman

74 · THE RESILIENT ACTOR

for the part, I didn't go. The casting director didn't find a Latina woman he liked in the auditions, so he hired a girl who happened to look just like me. I may have gotten that part, but I didn't even show up!

Don't limit yourself or talk yourself out of an audition. You may be more right for a part than you realize, and, even if you don't get the part, other good things can happen. They might not know what they're looking for until they see you, or you may change their minds. A director might decide to use you in another show, or he might like you so much that he writes in a part for you. Never pass up an opportunity to get in front of people with casting authority unless, of course, you're sick or woefully unprepared. You never know who's in the room or who they could become. You don't know what can happen, but you'll never know if you don't show up.

Here's the main reason many of us don't go to auditions: our minds tell us every reason not to go. Our minds can be jerks like that. Our delicate egos are happy in that comfort zone and don't want to give anyone the chance to bruise it. "Stay home!" say our egos, "Stay home where it's safe! We'll eat potato chips and watch Netflix!" That little voice will talk you out of anything that moves you closer to your goals, so you need to tell that voice to shut the hell up.

That's your immature voice, and you're a grownup.

Grownups do what they need to do whether they feel like it or not. Tell that little voice to take a flying leap. You've got big plans that don't involve the couch, television, or ice cream. We're adulting.

If that jerk in your head is super loud and you need help, then vocalize your intentions. Saying it out loud or telling someone can make its protests sound silly and dissipate them. Take the power out of it.

Tell another actor that you'll meet them at the audition, then you have to go. You can also have an accountability buddy, an actor friend who goes along with you. Auditioning is more fun with a carpool pal and the time passes faster when someone stands in line with you. You might be standing in line a *long* time. Your buddy might be able to stand outside the door during your audition and give you feedback later. You can do the same for them.

The more auditions you go to, the more people you'll meet in the community, and the more friendly faces you'll see at future auditions. Go and do a great job, but have fun, too. The fact is, unless you get a part in a long-running show (and those are rare), you need to audition often.

Reward yourself for auditions. If it's a hard one to show up for, after it's done, go to that movie you've been wanting to see or buy that beautiful sweater for yourself, *but only if you go to the audition first.*

ONWARD AND UPWARD

Don't get hung up on the negative feelings you have from past auditions. One of my favorite authors, Dr. Rick Hanson, writes about mindfulness, meditation, and presence. One of his ideas about negativity can be applied to auditions. People have a bias toward negativity. When something negative happens, our brains imprint it immediately. That survival instinct was useful when we had to worry about hungry saber-toothed tigers. A negative experience imprints on us so that if we do something that could kill us, we remember it, and won't put ourselves in that situation again. Today, we don't have to worry about tigers. But if we get rejected for a role, it sticks—immediately.

A positive experience takes longer to imprint on our memories. A compliment from a friend may be pleasant, but it won't save your life. Our brains, with their old design, aren't as quick to remember those positive experiences. This worked out well for the survival of the species, but it doesn't work out so well for keeping us motivated for auditions today.

Make an effort to find the good in every audition. Call a friend and talk to them about those things. Don't let the fact that you didn't get a part be the only thing you remember. Dwell on the good stuff. Did you make a new friend? Did you get to show yourself to a new casting director or producer? Did you get a tip on another audition? Did you get a high compliment or some good feedback that you can use in your next audition? Be grateful for all of that. Think about it, talk about it, and write it down. Dwell on the good things. Those memories aren't going to stick if you don't make them stick. Use them to put you in the right mindset for your next audition—and stop getting in your own way. You'll look forward to every audition and every new challenge in your life.

The healthier you are going into an audition, the easier it'll be to take on the challenge and survive rejection. Being healthy will get you through many auditions, and we'll talk about that in depth in Scene 4. But first, we have some business to take care of: the business of the business.

WHAT CAN I DO TODAY?

Preparing for auditions is an ongoing process. If you're not prepared, you won't go to enough auditions to have an acting career. The following are questions you can answer and exercises you can do to get you to more auditions:

- What happened at your last audition? Make a list of all the good things that came out of that audition, then call a friend and tell them all about it. After your next audition, make a new list. Imprint the positives of every audition on your psyche.

- Are you prepared for your next audition? Even if you don't have one lined up, prepare. Pack a bag, pick out an outfit, and prepare a monologue or some old sides. Find one success ritual and practice it. Do a little every day and you'll be more prepared and excited for your next audition.

- How often do you look for auditions? Where do you look for them? If you have a talent agent, how often do you call them? Do you look for work yourself? Find at least three websites that post auditions and subscribe to them. Read the breakdowns weekly. Find an audition today and put it on your calendar.

THE BUSINESS OF THE BUSINESS

Read your pay stub closely. There are many honest producers and general managers out there. But many of them are also willing to take full advantage of you. Watch out for yourself and remember that it's a business, and commercial theatre is one of the best and worst places to be an actor. If you have a thick skin and are willing to stand up for yourself, you'll be okay.

—SPENCER MOSES, *SCHOOL OF ROCK, ZHIVAGO, GUYS & DOLLS,* BROADWAY, CO-STARRING ROLES ON *NURSE JACKIE, PERSON OF INTEREST, BOARDWALK EMPIRE*

Working behind the scenes in the Hollywood film and television industry was fascinating. I met interesting, powerful people and learned how decisions were made.

That part of my career was also disillusioning. I learned

that the most talented writers, directors, actors, and even Hollywood executives don't always get the job. Sometimes clueless, less-talented people get hired because their dad got them the job or because they're attractive or connected. Unless your mom or dad is a big Hollywood producer (and often even then) you're going to have to hustle for work.

GET YOUR HUSTLE ON

Don't wait to be invited to audition. If you want a job...go after it. If your agent can't get you in, go to the open call. I auditioned for Sacramento Music Circus for fourteen years before they cast me. Never did I ever decide, "They don't like me; I'll never get in there." I just kept auditioning. We really all have nothing but time, and you're a different age, talent, human with each passing year...so keep presenting the new you until someone buys it!

—BETS MALONE, *THE MARVELOUS WONDERETTES,* OFF-BROADWAY; *BARBIE AS THE ISLAND PRINCESS, WHAT'S WRONG WITH RUTH?*

Our clients at the talent agency were as big as they come. All the multi-million-dollar movie stars were there. Agents hustled to get work for the talent they represented. Managers hustled to make sure the agents did their jobs. Managers would call agents and ask, "Did you submit so-and-so for this part? What about this part?" Even Meryl Streep—who has more Oscars and more Oscar nominations than any of us will ever dream of—had a team of people hustling to find her new roles. Of course, she gets sent a mountain of scripts, but most of them are crap. Even people in high demand understand that acting is a business. Getting work is a continuous process. They hustle or pay someone to hustle for them. That perfect script isn't going to be hand-delivered to their door by script fairies.

Hustle is tenaciously leaning forward and actively working toward your goal. It's a strong work ethic, and doing the work that needs to be done with a brisk, aggressive pace. I don't mean the unethical, scammy connotation of the word. Think basketball, not back alley.

Have you ever seen a good, famous actor in a bad, what-were-they-thinking movie? I used to wonder why actors did movies like that. Then I realized that sometimes even A-list actors accept roles just to pay the bills. The mortgage is due, or they just got divorced and have to pay alimony. Even when there are no good parts available, actors still need to work. They might fork out 10 or 20 percent of their pay to an agent, a manager, a publicist, and an attorney. Sometimes they're lucky to keep even half of their salary. They need to work to keep generating income.

You need to work too, and you can't rely on your agent to get you work all the time. Unless you're Leonardo DiCaprio or Anna Kendrick nobody is going to beg you to be in their film—you have to be proactive. If you have an agent or a manager, you have to make sure they're doing their jobs without hassling them. You can't sit back and wait for them to call. You have to be out there hustling and know what's going on in the business every day. Get out there and build relationships with people who can help you get hired.

AGENTS AND AGENCIES

You might be tempted to sign with the biggest agency that will represent you, but that can be a mistake when you're first starting out. If you're represented by a huge agency, you're a guppy swimming with whales. No one will notice you. Big agencies represent major talent, and your agent won't spend much time on you. They'll focus on the people who make them the most money. Ten percent of $40 million is a lot more than 10 percent of scale (the Screen Actors Guild minimum wage). Everyone has to make a profit, and they want to make as much as possible. Sure, some agents care about putting clients in artistic roles that advance their career, but more often, it's about making money.

Your relationship with your agent is like a marriage. You have to find someone who really gets your "thing." Even if it's a smaller agency, hold out until you can find the perfect mate.

It took me two agencies and a period of time being without one until I found the one that really understood what made me unique.

—DAVE THOMAS BROWN, *AMERICAN PSYCHO*, BROADWAY; *THE LEGEND OF GEORGIA MCBRIDE, HEATHERS*, OFF-BROADWAY; *BRIDGES OF MADISON COUNTY*, FIRST NATIONAL TOUR

Go with a smaller agency that'll give you the attention you need to get started. At first, you won't get the attention you feel you deserve. Once you prove to your agent that you can make them some money, they'll spend more time getting you seen. You can overcome that dilemma by getting out there and getting yourself some work. Finding your own gigs gives you the opportunity to look for better roles, too. Usually, but not always, your agent is more interested in getting you booked in anything so they can get paid. They're less interested in driving your career.

I can't stress enough the importance of being proactive about your career. The truth is, actors of all levels are always hustling to stay employed. If they're not auditioning, they're meeting with directors. They're lunching with producers and having dinner with other actors. Network like a beast to stay competitive. Get in front of people who can hire you.

The best time to get an agent is when you already have work, which, I know, is a catch-22. The idea is to be able to

demonstrate that you are capable of making them lots of money—if you can book on your own, imagine what you could do with them?

—ERIN CRONICAN, THE ACTORS' ENTERPRISE

Keep your headshots current. Your headshots should look like you now, not ten years ago. Headshot styles change, so know what the current trend is and make sure yours aren't out of date. Everyone used to have 8 x 10 glossy black and white photos, but now they're all in color. You can find out what the current trends are by talking to photographers. Go into places that print headshots and look at the photos and visit other actors' websites. Headshots that are current and in style cost time and money, but that's part of the job. It's an investment you have to make in your career.

Create and maintain a good resume. You can download a template to help you get started, or have a friend help you create one. There are companies that'll create a professional resume for you if you want to spend the money. Format it so it's easy to read and include up-to-date acting credits. Don't exaggerate, make stuff up, or misrepresent yourself at all on your resume. Don't include information that might cast you in a bad light, either. Leave off your home address, other than city and state, for safety reasons. You don't want unwanted guests showing up on your doorstep. Once you have a nice-looking resume, update it every time you get new work. A headshot and resume may be the first impression a casting director has of you. Make sure those materials reflect your best you. Take your time to do it right.

If you need help getting a website together, my friend Amy Russ runs a great company called www.actorswebs.com. They help actors design and maintain professional websites.

BE CHILI

Your headshots and resume should represent your best self and they should also be true to who you are. Be honest about how you represent yourself to casting directors. If you're chili, be chili. What does that mean? Figure out who you are: What's your type, and what kinds of roles are right for you? Be honest. Are you the girl-next-door type or the bossy neighbor? Are you a street punk, a bookworm, or a good-looking leading man or woman?

Think about this like advertising, the packaging of a product. If you're spicy chili with beans, then put that on the label. If you put filet mignon on the label and the casting director opens the package and gets spicy chili with beans, he'll be pissed. If he orders chili and gets steak, he won't be happy either. Put roles on your resume that represent your type. Have headshots that look like you. Everything about your package should represent you accurately so a director knows what he's getting. If you're chili, be chili, and if you're filet mignon, be filet mignon. The caveat here is that you don't have to limit yourself to one type of chili. Your headshots and roles may show varieties of you. You can be chili with steak, chili with cheese—even Cincinnati three-way chili (which, by the way, is a weird spaghetti with meat sauce dish).

That image you have of yourself may be wrong or outdated. Think about the roles you auditioned for and got a callback or were cast. Are there roles you played and got a big response? Think about the times when someone said to you, "That's a *perfect* part for you."

Ask your friends and teachers who they think you are and when you've been at your best. Compile a list of those parts and focus on where you fit in the acting world. Have audition material, headshots, and a resume that show off that best part of you. Be you. Authentic you. The clearer you are about what you bring to the table, the easier it is to sell yourself in the acting market.

What you discover may surprise you. You may not be who you thought you were, but you need to accept it. At my age, I no longer play the ingénue. I may be able to act the part and sing those roles to my heart's content, but my role now is playing everybody's mom. I play the best mom I can—chili with beans! Accept who you are and be the best version of that person. You'll get more roles and be better in them.

DO YOUR HOMEWORK

Acting requires regular research to keep abreast of what's going on. Look up other actors' headshots and resumes to see what they look like and what they're doing. Know what shows are playing and watch clips of them online. Read breakdowns and see what all the theaters are doing. What about television pilots? What's in audition and in production now? Which studios are producing them? Which directors are working on what films?

Part of being in the business is knowing what shows are coming down the pike. Read the trades and websites like the Actors' Equity site, which posts auditions for theater productions all over the country. You have to be a member to view the listings, but you can view them by region or city. Read theater websites and subscribe to their emailing lists to get regular updates. Join a local actor's co-op or organization. Some offer classes and you can meet with other actors to talk about auditions.

Check sites like *Backstage* for casting calls. *Variety* and *Hollywood Reporter* focus on the business, but you can read them to find out who the players are and what projects are in the works. You can get clues about who's casting, what's in production, and who the people are that you need to know. The more you know about the business, the more opportunities you'll discover. Understand the industry so you can discuss it when you're out with friends or at a party. You never know who you might meet and it will give you something to talk about. If you live in a big industry city like L.A. or New York, you have a high likelihood of running into people in the industry. That girl sitting next to you at the coffee shop in a t-shirt and yoga pants could be an up-and-coming director.

In addition to the main audition websites (Actors Access, Backstage, LA Casting, etc.), you also want to read industry trades daily, like Variety, The Hollywood Reporter, Playbill, IMDB—sometimes you'll see things mentioned in interviews that will give you a head start on projects. Plus, you'll be more "in the know" when you have conversations with colleagues.

—ERIN CRONICAN, THE ACTORS' ENTERPRISE

Read scripts. You can get scripts for free at the library and online, or buy them at bookstores and online. Trade scripts with your friends. Carry a script with you wherever you go so you can read it while you're waiting at the diner or riding the subway. Get a play or screenplay reading group together to meet in your living room and read through scripts. Reading and acting with other actors is good practice to keep your chops up.

NOBODY WANTS TO TAKE A CHANCE ON YOU— AT FIRST

If you're already working, congratulations, you can skip this part! If you're new to the business, or to a different area of the business, prepare yourself for an uphill battle to get that first job. Booking your first role can be harder than actually doing the job. You're an untested actor and directors are reluctant to take a chance on you. They'd rather another casting director take that risk. Once you get your foot in the door it's easier to keep the door open for future work.

If you pay your dues and prepare, have the talent and tenacity, and keep showing up, you'll get booked. Then something magical will happen. The more work you get, the more work you'll get. Work begets work. People will see you working and want to hire you. Stick it out and someone will take that risk and then you'll be a working actor.

Casting directors aren't just mean and stingy with the roles. They want to find new talent, but they also have to consider the business side of the business. Productions—films, commercials, musicals, plays—cost a LOT of money to produce. When directors cast you for a role, they're making an investment. Before they spend a dime, they want to know you're not a bad investment. They want to know you're going to be reliable and that you're going to show up when you say you're going to show up. Many people put their time, money, and artistic hearts into these projects. They want to be sure you're a team player who'll do well for everybody involved in the production.

An actor's reputation precedes them. If you have a good work ethic—no, let's make that an excellent work ethic—the folks behind the table will be talking about that right before you enter the room. If there has been any "drama" in the past, that WILL be the topic of conversation. Think of all the work you have done to prep for this audition. If this is the talk behind the table, it's a no-win situation.

—COURTNEY COREY, FOUNDER AND DIRECTOR
OF THEATRE ARTS SCHOOL OF SAN DIEGO

Do everything you can to make it easy for directors to say yes to you, and don't give them any reasons to say no. Be nice to everybody, including understudies, assistants, the stage manager, *everybody*. You don't know who those people are or who they know. You don't know who they're sleeping with, or who they may become someday. Maybe the assistant called in sick and the person you think is the assistant is actually the director. She could be the production stage manager for the show. If you're rude and you still somehow get the part, you'll have to make up for that awful first impression.

Every job is an interview for the next job. The person handing you a prop, sitting next to you in the dressing room, opposite you on stage or hitting you with a spotlight could one day give you a job. So being kind, professional, and helpful to EVERY-ONE in the building will come back to serve you down the line.

—BETS MALONE, *THE MARVELOUS WONDERETTES*, OFF-BROADWAY; *BARBIE AS THE ISLAND PRINCESS, WHAT'S WRONG WITH RUTH?*

When you're just starting out, you have to pay your dues. Audition *often*. Audition for smaller roles and for student films. Acting in a student film at NYU (or Okeechobee Community College) beats not working and gives you an acting credit for your resume.

Don't just focus on the money. A role that doesn't pay well (or at all) may be worthwhile if there's another payoff. Whenever I'm lucky enough to have more than one role offered to me, I consider what I have to gain from each. Beyond the cash, will the role expand my resume? Will it involve a director, actor, writer, or anyone else I'd like to work with? Is it an artistically satisfying part? If it is, then I'm more inclined to overlook the fact that it's a smaller role—or paycheck.

HIT YOUR MARK, NO MATTER HOW BIG OR SMALL

If you get a small role or are cast in an obscure film or play, don't phone in your performance. Give it your best.

There's an old expression, "It's always somebody's first show and somebody's last show." Never take your audience for granted. Perform as if it's someone's first experience in the theater or the last show someone will see before they die. With DVDs and the internet, nothing on film goes away forever. Give them your best version of you and use the opportunity to hone your skills. Plus, you never know who's in the audience, and people with casting authority do go to small shows. Bring your A game. Keep your ego in check, even if it feels like the gig is beneath you.

When you're working, people want to hire you. When you're not working, you're a tougher sell. Work hard and pay your dues. At some point, you'll have the experience for bigger roles, and you'll be worth the risk.

When you think you are working hard, know that there is someone working harder.

When you think you want that role, know that there is someone who wants it more.

—COURTNEY COREY, FOUNDER AND DIRECTOR
OF THEATRE ARTS SCHOOL OF SAN DIEGO

WHAT CAN I DO TODAY?

Acting is the perk, and today is about the work. Ask yourself these questions and spend a little time on each exercise. If you spend just a couple of hours a week on the business of the business, you'll make progress.

- What's your type? What roles are right for you? Look at your past roles and talk to your acting teacher, voice coach, and friends. Get some clarity and then look at your headshots, resume, and audition material. Do they represent who you are as an actor? If they don't, update them.
- What's going on in the acting world in your area? Do you know what shows are auditioning and which ones are in production? What are the local studios doing? Find websites and magazines to read and events to attend related to the business of the business. Ask one of your acting buddies to attend an opening with you and make it a monthly event.
- What scripts are you reading? Get a library card and see what your library has to offer. Ask your friends if they have any scripts they can loan you. Make a habit of carrying a script with you at all times and read it. Consider starting a weekly reading group with your actor friends. Call one of them right now and see if they're interested.

SCENE 4

FINE-TUNING YOUR INSTRUMENT / PHYSICAL RESILIENCE

Performing artists are the only artists that use their bodies as instruments, so you really need to get to know yourself. Treat your body like a machine that needs to be finely tuned to operate optimally.

—ERIN CRONICAN, THE ACTORS' ENTERPRISE

You're poring over the trades, learning lines, and auditioning. You're trying your best to make sound business decisions about your career. You're giving yourself to your audience every night and on every shoot.

You need energy, mental acuity, and resilience to bring your best game every single day. How do you stay sharp for all the demands?

It all starts with your instrument. You are the instrument. You are the cello, the flute, the piano—and you have to stay in tune. As actors, we have to keep ourselves in top form to thrive!

ENERGY MANAGEMENT: CHARGERS AND DRAINERS

Balancing organization and managing time and energy is a huge part of the game of the arts. Eating healthy, sleeping, exercising and having YOU time makes a huge difference in day-to-day life. For me, taking various classes—from yoga, hip-hop dance class and spinning to kickboxing—shakes up my routine and keeps me on my feet. They all serve a purpose in my craft. Each class teaches me a range of concentration, focus and release that applies to acting.

—ALLISON SPRATT PEARCE, *CURTAINS, CRY BABY, GOOD VIBRATIONS*, BROADWAY; WWW.ALLISONSPRATTPEARCE.COM

As I got my health, career, and lifestyle in balance, I learned a simple trick to manage and maximize my energy—dividing my habits and routines into two categories: chargers and drainers.

Chargers rev up your energy and increase health, energy, and resilience. They make you feel amazing—invincible! Drainers sap your energy, hold you back, and make you feel like crap. Chargers help you kick ass, while drainers can kick your ass. My coaching mentor, Dave Asprey, describes drainers as kryptonite, the mineral that sapped Superman himself.

The *real* trick is identifying your own chargers and filling your life with them, then figuring out what your drainers are so you can avoid them.

Chargers and drainers come in all shapes and sizes. They can be the food you eat, activities you do, people you hang out with, and even how you sleep. Some chargers are obvious, like washing your hands and brushing your teeth. Other chargers are more complicated and kind of...out there. Cryotherapy, flotation tanks, sophisticated supplementation, meditation, tai chi, and deeper levels of therapy fall into that category.

Likewise, we can pick off the obvious drainers, like junk food, too much alcohol, and staying up all night. But there are also hidden drainers in our lives that suck our energy without us being aware of them.

Energy management is about figuring out what you can do to boost your energy to be the best actor and human you can be. Let's start with the big three: sleep, nutrition, and exercise.

SLEEP

Rest. Performers often ask for "remedies" when their voices are shot and their energy is down. Resting will help the body heal. It's better than any magic pill or potion. That being said, schedule rest into your busy weeks, like tech week. Get a good night's sleep each night and find a moment during the day to chill for a bit.

—COURTNEY COREY, FOUNDER AND DIRECTOR
OF THEATRE ARTS SCHOOL OF SAN DIEGO

The most important thing we can do for our health—and the hardest with our schedules—is sleep. Most people need eight hours of sleep every night, but some of us need less and some need more. Most of us don't get enough quality sleep. We try to make up for it with caffeine and energy drinks that turn us into tired, wired walking zombies. You can function (not thrive) on a lousy diet and no exercise, but you need sleep to survive.

Necessary housekeeping goes on in your body and your mind while you're asleep. If you shortchange yourself in sleep hours, you'll never be as healthy as you could be. Your body needs that downtime to recharge and clean out the trash. The glymphatic system, your built-in detox system, does that while you sleep. We rest, recharge, clean out our bodies, integrate experiences, and more in our sleep.

Track Your ZZZs

I also make sure to have as steady of a wake up time and sleep time as possible so I get enough sleep for energy and weight control!

—ADI MULLEN, ACTOR/DANCER, *SPRING AWAKENING,*
CYGNET THEATRE; *FESTIVAL OF CHRISTMAS:*
NORTHERN LIGHTS, LAMB'S PLAYERS THEATRE

Find out how much sleep you need to feel rested. You can use sleep tracking software and apps, or just pay attention to how you feel every morning and write it down.

I use a Beddit sleep tracker device on my mattress; better yet, I love my ŌURA Ring, which tells me detailed information about deep, REM, and light sleep cycles, as well as my wakeup patterns. It also tracks steps, heart rate, heart rate variability, respiration, body temperature, and more. A phone app like Sleep Cycle analyzes your sleep and the alarm wakes you up when you're in a lighter sleep stage in the morning. Some Fitbits can track sleep as well. If you track it, you can start to detect what your sleep drainers might be.

You can also start a sleep journal. If you wake up feeling like you got hit by a truck, obviously there's a problem. Write down what you did the day and night before, and how you felt when you woke up. On a morning when you felt like crap, did you have three glasses of wine the night before? Did you feel better in the morning when you skipped that late night TV show and got to bed an hour earlier? Notice how you feel every morning and give yourself a score from 1 to 10, then write down what you did the previous day. After a while, you'll see patterns. You'll know which activities to include in your daily life, and which to curb or cut out completely.

I need eight hours of sleep, which is a challenge with three kids and a career. When I'm in a show or rehearsing, I often don't get to bed until midnight, but my kids are wide awake at 6 a.m.! I can't function well on six hours of sleep, so I schedule time in those days to get extra rest through napping, meditation, or some of the sleep hacks I'll discuss later in this chapter. That might mean skipping a yoga class or turning down a lunch invitation, but sleep must be a priority for me. An after-lunch nap works best when I'm already starting to feel fatigued after a busy morning. In some countries, it's still customary to take a midday nap or siesta. This is in line with natural circadian rhythms. If you know you're going to have a day with a sleep shortage, schedule a nap ahead of time.

When should you sleep, and how much sleep do you need? Research shows that most people sleep best between 10 p.m. and 6 a.m. Our deepest, most restful and rejuvenating sleep happens before 2 a.m. Our best dreaming and mental and emotional integration happens between 2 a.m. and 7 a.m. To get in enough sleep cycles of all stages of sleep, most people need about eight hours of sleep every night.

Everyone is different. We each have our own chronotype, or the propensity to sleep or be alert at a particular time of day. Some people are early risers, and some people are at their best in the wee hours. Dr. Michael Breus illustrates these chronotypes in his book The Power of When, and his free online quiz at www.thepowerofwhenquiz.com can help you figure out your chronotype. (Just for the record, like the majority of people, I'm a bear.)

If you're in a show or shooting late on set, it's tough to get to bed by 10 o'clock. On the nights you can, go to bed by 10 p.m. On nights when you're working late, go to bed as early as you can or keep your morning clear to catch it on the morning end. Try to keep a consistent sleep schedule.

Sleep Drainers

Be aware of your sleep drainers. Then, reduce or remove those activities from your daily routines. That third glass of wine may knock you out, but you won't sleep as deeply. Coffee late in the day can also keep you awake. Track how late you're drinking caffeinated beverages and how they affect your sleep. It's a good rule of thumb to avoid caffeine eight hours before you go to bed (2 p.m. is my cutoff). If you're sensitive to caffeine, you may need to have your last cup of coffee, caffeinated tea, or energy drinks even earlier in the day.

Prepare yourself and your room for sleep. Avoid electronic screens one to two hours before bedtime. The blue light from our phones, computers, and televisions suppresses the melatonin—the happy hormone that tells our brains it's nighttime and helps us sleep. Our brain doesn't know the difference between an iPhone and the sun. When you're staring at your phone, it thinks it's daytime and keeps you awake.

If you have to use a screen at night, wear blue blocker sunglasses or use a screen filter that alters the color of the light. Your computer and phone may have a night shift or color filter setting that reduces the blue light, or you can download software like f.lux or Iris that does this too.

Make your bedroom cool and dark. Between sixty and sixty-eight degrees in your bedroom is the ideal sleeping temperature. Put blackout curtains on the windows or wear an eye mask. Cover glowing lights from electronics with a bit of electrical tape. If you live in a noisy neighborhood, put on some white noise or gentle music to drown it out and help you relax. Try to make it as cool, quiet, and dark as possible. Think cave.

Put your phone on airplane mode or turn it off completely

so you're not awaked by every buzz, bleep, or beep. Reduce the electromagnetic field (EMF) pollution in your room. You don't want to zap your brain with electricity and cell phone waves while you're asleep. Put your iPhone and its charger across the room, not under your pillow. Ideally, turn off your Wi-Fi in your house or bedroom completely at night. You can put your router on a timer or unplug it when you head to bed. This way you are not bathed in all that EMF pollution while you rest.

Sleep Chargers

Likewise, add more sleep chargers to your daily routines. It's tough to wind down after a late night performance, so develop a ritual that puts you in the right state of mind. A bath, a cup of herbal tea, some journaling or light reading can help you relax. Avoid stimulating food, drink, activities, or people in the last hour before bed.

Meditation can relax your body and your mind and help you sleep better. Exercise also helps you sleep better, just don't exercise too late in the day, which can have the opposite effect and keep you awake. If you're plagued by thoughts at bedtime, try journaling. Write in your workbook, download your thoughts to your roommate, or record a voice memo on your phone to clear your mind. Take a warm bath with Epsom salt or try herbs and essential oils to help you relax. Melatonin, valerian, chamomile, and lavender oil might put you in a more restful mood.

If you need a pick-me-up during the day, have a small coffee or use deep breathing or movement. But don't depend on caffeine to make up for sleep shortages on a regular basis. Just like you can't exercise your way out of a bad diet in a day, you can't caffeinate your way out of sleep deprivation.

If you suspect that you have sleep apnea or another disorder, consult a doctor. Hidden health factors like adrenal fatigue or even parasites can mess with your sleep. Once you know how much sleep you need and how to get it, make sleeping a priority. You can't be your best self without sleep.

NUTRITION

After sleep, proper nutrition is the most important charger you can give yourself. Humans are like giant walking chemistry sets. We're big bags of water and chemicals, and what we add to the mix affects how we feel and behave. You can manage how you feel and act by understanding how the food you eat affects you. Then, identify your nutrition chargers and drainers so you can make better food choices.

For years we were taught that fat was the enemy. Some fats are still bad for you, like trans fats, hydrogenated fats, and some vegetable oils, but many fats are essential to a healthy diet. The fats your grandmother used to eat, like good quality butter and tallow aren't bad for you. When we started believing all fat was bad, food corporations took the fat out. Unfortunately, they replaced it with ingredients that *are* bad for us, like sugar and chemicals. The result was obesity and diabetes in record numbers. Fat and some cholesterol are necessary for our bodies to produce hormones. We need this stuff in our diets to have nutritional balance and feel good. Even the American Heart Association has reversed its recommendations about cholesterol and fat. If you aren't getting enough healthy animal fat in your diet, consider taking a fish oil supplement, or choose a vegetarian option like olive oil or coconut oil. Fat will keep you satiated and help you resist sugar and refined carbs. Eating healthy fat will help your willpower.

Nutrition Chargers

Veggies, preferably organic vegetables, should take up the most room on your plate. Eat your vegetables—not your fruits and vegetables—but your vegetables, especially the green, leafy ones. They're nutritious and fill you up. They contain the most vitamins, phytonutrients, and antioxidants. Do I need to continue telling you that vegetables are good for you?

Fruit is a different matter. Sure, it grows on trees and is delicious and nutritious. But most fruit is like a bag of water and sugar (in the form of fructose) with a little bit of nutrition. Be selective about how much and what types of fruit you eat. I have a few berries when they're in season. And I rarely drink fruit juice at all (except for the occasional Mimosa) because it's like guzzling a concentrated fruit bomb of sugar and carbohydrates. Go easy on the fruit.

Quality protein is necessary for a healthy diet. Stick to wild fish and grass-fed/grass-finished, pasture raised, high-quality protein. Taco Bell and McDonald's protein doesn't count. Have a moderate amount of protein daily, starting with about half a gram to one gram per pound of body weight. Too much protein will raise your insulin and your body will turn the extra protein into blood sugar and body fat. Buy the best quality protein you can afford and keep a food diary to track your protein intake.

Carbohydrates are controversial. I eat some rice or sweet potatoes with my dinner, but in small amounts and not every day. We need fewer carbohydrates than the government pyramid would lead us to believe, and we definitely do not need refined carbs like flour, sugar, cookies, chips, and doughnuts. Eat real food and minimize carbs. The more active you are, the more carbohydrates you can consume. A good nutritionist or health coach can guide you through maintaining a healthy balance of the right carbs in your diet.

I'm just scratching the surface on this controversial topic of diet. A good rule of thumb for most people is to fill your plate with a generous portion of veggies, dressed with some good fats, a little high-quality protein, and a few complex carbs.

Nutrition Drainers

You don't have to be allergic to a food to be affected by it. When I eat gluten, it doesn't cause me to have an anaphylactic reaction. But, I know how it makes me feel—tired, foggy-brained, and gassy—and I feel much, *much* better without it. Why would I eat something that makes me feel crappy? Certain foods can cause inflammation and indigestion. Common foods that cause reactions include gluten, dairy, eggs, nuts, and soy. Some people also react to legumes and nightshade foods like tomatoes, peppers, and eggplant.

To test your sensitivity, cut all foods you think might be causing issues for you, and then add them back one at a time. Journal your diet and see if there are correlations between the foods you eat and how you feel. When you remove dairy from your diet for a few days, then drink a glass of milk, does your nose get stuffy? Does your throat get scratchy or does your skin break out? Do onions make you super gassy? You may not be allergic to certain foods, but if they cause unpleasant side effects, why eat them?

My biggest food drainer is sugar. It metabolizes quickly and makes me cranky. When I eat a little sugar, I want all the sugar in the world—it's just that addictive. Sugar makes you fat, ages you faster, causes inflammation, rots your teeth, and screws up your energy. Staying away from sugar was one of the most beneficial lessons I learned in getting healthy. Replace that sugar with healthy fats to reduce cravings.

I didn't realize how much sugar was hurting me until I stopped eating it. I stopped wanting it, lost weight, and felt better. My mood swings went away and I wasn't a cranky bitch (well, except for once a month). Whenever I ate sugar, I became shaky and unstable. If I didn't eat something else right away, I'd blow up. Now, without sugar, if I miss a meal, I'm okay. It took some work for me to give up sugar because it's in so many processed and prepared foods. After I stopped eating it for about three days it got easier. Hang on for three days.

Table sugar is easy to identify, but what about hidden

sugars and foods that turn into sugar when they're digested? Sugar occurs naturally in fruits and is often added to processed foods, so I aim for zero sugar and end up with trace amounts of it. Refined carbohydrates, flour, and even too much fruit will give you a sugar rush. You don't want to eliminate carbohydrates completely from your diet. Eat fewer of them, stick to complex carbohydrates, and eat foods that also have fiber in them—you'll feel much better.

I also avoid foods made with wheat (all forms of gluten) and I believe most people would be better off without it. The wheat we ate many years ago has been modified so much that it isn't easily digestible for many people. It can cause health problems like allergies, leaky gut, digestive disturbances, and autoimmune conditions. Some research suggests that glyphosate—a pesticide sprayed on wheat—is also harmful, and may be the true cause of wheat allergies. Think about excluding wheat from your diet and going gluten free. Your digestive problems, brain fog, and other chronic inflammation may disappear. There are plenty of other grains to eat. Just don't go hog wild on gluten-free, processed foods. Just because they're gluten free doesn't mean they're "all-you-can-eat." Just because they're gluten free doesn't mean they're healthy.

Maintaining a healthy diet at home is one thing, but what about when you're on tour? Plan ahead by Googling healthy restaurants or health food stores located at your destination. You can also have Amazon ship healthy snacks to your next stop so they're waiting for you.

Digestion

Digestion is how food breaks down in your body. Enzymes in your saliva and gastrointestinal (GI) tract are necessary for proper digestion. Like your grandmother used to say, take one bite at a time, chew your food slowly, and swallow before you take that next bite. Let the enzymes do their job—and don't talk with your mouth full.

We tend to produce less acid in our stomachs as we age, so I supplement with HCL (hydrochloric acid) and digestive enzymes. Don't fall into the trap of taking antacids, because you need stomach acid to break down your food. If you need to add a supplement, talk to your doctor or nutritionist about your options. Find out what's going on with your diet (and your gut) and fix it.

Probiotics are popular for a good reason. Bacteria in our bodies assist with digestion, make neurotransmitters, help us assimilate our nutrients, and regulate mood. They probably do more that science hasn't even discovered yet. We should treat them well. I suggest everyone use a probiotic supplement. Eat probiotic foods every day to support the bacteria. Yogurt rarely has enough cultures.

Try good-quality, fermented sources like sauerkraut, kimchi, or kombucha. When you spend the money to eat the highest-quality food, you want to be sure your body is getting the most from it. Pay attention to not just what you eat, but how you digest it. Gut health is super important; it's one of the foundations of our good health.

Alcohol

For many people, alcohol is also part of the mix in that big chemistry set we call our bodies. Alcohol affects how we feel and behave. That may be especially true for people whose schedules end late at night (I'm looking at you, actor). Alcohol ages you, makes you tired, and impairs your sleep. If you choose to imbibe, pace yourself and limit your drinks. Alternate a glass of water with alcoholic beverages so you don't drink too fast or get dehydrated. Fruity drinks are loaded with sugar and calories, and creamy concoctions might have sugar and milk in them. Carbonated drinks or bubbly champagne at night might make you feel worse in the morning than beer or wine. Choose your drinks carefully and don't overdo it. There's nothing worse than going to an audition or a rehearsal with a hangover or not enough sleep. You'll suffer from both if you don't limit your alcohol intake.

I'm not saying don't drink. I'm saying drink smart. There are also some supplements you can take to metabolize alcohol better and not get as bad a hangover.

As you journal your meals and notice how you feel, you'll begin to discover correlations. You'll identify your food chargers and drainers. Maybe you had a bowl of corn flakes with milk, and an hour later you were cranky and hungry and wanted to eat all the doughnuts at craft services. Then your energy dropped, so you ate a triple burrito with salsa and onions. Later you felt even more sluggish, so you went to bed early and had horrible dreams that night. The effects may not be immediate. Sometimes the reaction could come a few days later. Journaling will help you figure out which foods cause certain reactions. Eating tomatoes (for example) may make your fingers bloat and give you headaches—two days later. If you haven't kept a food diary you may not remember eating them.

Apps like MyFitnessPal and Cronometer.com track what you eat and tell you how much of it's protein, carbs, and fats. You can track your nutrition, and use it as a food diary. That way, if you have a food reaction, you can check your meal history to see if there's a correlation. Or, you can just write it down on paper.

Supplements

Even the best diet may leave you undernourished. Nutrients have been depleted from the soil where our food is grown. Grains have been altered, and fruits and vegetables are often picked before they're ripe. Supplements can help make up for the nutrients that are lacking in the food you eat.

Don't dismiss the importance of nutritional supplements or think you don't need them. You may be so used to feeling tired and worn down that you don't realize you could feel amazing if you were properly nourished.

With supplements, you get what you pay for. Cheap drugstore vitamins can be low quality and packed with fillers. Read the labels. Do some research and find the best vitamins and supplements.

Although I'm a certified health coach and have given some general supplement recommendations here, supplementation should be personalized. I can't provide individual advice to a wide audience. You'll have to do your homework to determine what supplements you need in your diet. Companies like SpectraCell offer tests for vitamin, mineral, and antioxidant levels and deficiencies. Once you have that information, you can zero in on where your diet is lacking and what supplements you need. In particular, Vitamin D and magnesium deficiencies are common.

Ask a Pro

Your traditional family MD may have limited training in

nutrition. Nontraditional health care providers can be another resource. They can also work with you to develop an optimal diet. Integrative medical specialists, functional medicine specialists, naturopaths, and nutritionists can help with food sensitivities. If you think you have a food allergy, consult an allergist and get tested. You can get food sensitivity tests to help you sleuth out your problem foods. Companies such as EverlyWell and Pinnertest can test you with just a finger prick of blood and send you a list of food you may want to avoid. Talk to a health coach, nutritionist, or functional medical doctor to figure out what nutrients you need and how to get them in food or supplements. Educate yourself and learn to eat right. You can't be a resilient actor without proper nutrition.

Start Today

If you can only make a few changes to your diet right now, start with eating a lot more vegetables. Add some high-quality protein and good amounts of quality fat. If you can't afford all the supplements you need, at least take a high-quality multivitamin every day.

There are many diet and nutrition books out there, and I'm just scratching the surface. I *could* write a 500-page chapter and bore you with all the scientific studies behind proper diet and nutrition, but if you want to learn more, there are tons of resources available. Being aware of how food impacts your health, energy, and mood is a big step. Continuous education will keep you in step with your specific nutritional needs.

My diet has evolved over the years. I was a vegetarian or vegan for twenty years. It will continue to evolve as more nutrition information is available and I learn more about how my body reacts to foods. I follow a cyclical, ketogenic version of the paleo diet. I eat healthy fats, vegetables, and quality protein. For me, it's a good balance that maintains my weight and keeps me energized, balanced, and happy. If you don't follow a specific diet, work toward adding more vegetables, moderate protein, and healthy fats to your low-carb meals. Eat quality, real food. For some people, food beliefs can be as sacred as their religious beliefs. Don't get too bogged down by dogma or labels (vegetarian, paleo, vegan, etc.). Eat whatever works for you and be flexible and open minded to what makes you feel healthy.

EXERCISE

Hundreds. Take a Pilates class and you will likely learn this awesome core exercise. Do it before every show to engage your core, lower your center of gravity, and bring focus to your powerhouse.

—COURTNEY COREY, FOUNDER AND DIRECTOR
OF THEATRE ARTS SCHOOL OF SAN DIEGO

Sleep well, eat right, and yes, get your exercise. What makes you a healthy person also makes you a healthy actor. The three categories of exercise are cardiovascular (cardio), strength training, and flexibility. If you're new to cardio, weight, or flexibility training or you have a medical condition, check with your doctor first.

Cardio

Old-school cardio was running on a treadmill for as long as you could, or doing endless aerobics in your leg warmers. Look up Jane Fonda's "feel the burn" on YouTube for a giggle. Gratefully, cardio is growing up. High-intensity interval training can meet your cardiovascular training needs so you don't have to spend hours on the treadmill, which can drain your adrenals and put stress on your body. Twenty minutes of running or high-intensity calisthenics three days a week is plenty. Unlike marathon workouts, interval training raises your heart rate without wearing you down. Pick something you can and will do, like running, rowing, or weight exercises. Push-ups, sit-ups, and Burpees work fine. Do a minute of intense exercise to make yourself breathless, take a minute to recover, and do another set. Keep going for twenty minutes. You can make the same cardiovascular gains in a shorter amount of time. If you don't already have a cardio regimen, find one online, download an app, or pick up a DVD to help you get started. Longer endurance runs or bike rides at a lower heart rate are fine to mix it up, but those endless hours at the gym aren't necessary. If you feel you aren't disciplined enough to stick to an exercise routine, take a class and get an accountability buddy to go with you. I like interval cardio mixed with weight training classes because they take the thinking out of what exercises—and how much—to do.

Strength Training

Weight training is important—and may be even more important for your health than cardio. Boost your metabolism, maintain muscle mass, gain the hormonal benefits, and show off that tight bod with weight work. But swinging one-pound dumbbells or lifting heavy barbells with poor form won't do your muscles any good, and you could injure yourself. There's a method to strength training, so before you get some weights, get some instruction. Learn how to strength train properly with kettlebells, dumbbells, or weight equipment at the gym so you're using weights that are heavy enough to build muscle while taxing your muscles safely.

Check with a trainer at the local gym or check out YouTube tutorials to help you get started. Alternate your cardio and weight training days, and give yourself rest days to recover.

Flexibility

Add flexibility or mobility training to your cardio and strength training routines. You can take a yoga class, get a DVD, or find an online class to learn the moves. Yoga helps with flexibility and balance and is a great stress reliever.

Stretch after your cardio and weight routines for faster and less painful recovery. After working out use a foam roller, fascia stick, tennis ball, or rolling pin to work out all the kinks.

Movement

Movement is different than working out. It's about being a more active person in general—not sitting. Our bodies are meant to move. If you're sitting at a desk most of the day, take regular breaks. Stand up and go for a walk or do a set of push-ups, sit-ups, or squats. If you're watching television, get up during the commercial breaks. Pause the show every twenty minutes and do some jumping jacks. Make movement part of your life. Actors have active careers (which is great), but with movement, more is more, so take a walk.

Living in a city like New York makes movement easy because you already walk everywhere. If you live in L.A. and depend on your car or Uber to get around town, you have to be more intentional about getting out there and walking. If you can't go for a walk, get up every hour and bounce around or shake your hands to get your circulation going.

Our bodies don't come loaded with energy—we have to get up and make energy. You must charge your own battery. Sitting on the couch doesn't give you energy. Eating right, getting enough sleep, and regular exercise will generate energy for you. You need that energy—a *lot* of energy—for your acting career.

DETOXIFICATION

Our bodies have processes for getting rid of all the garbage we put in them. Natural elimination worked well for many years. These days, we're bombarded with chemicals and pollution and can end up with more toxins than our bodies can handle. The trash gets backed up and that can lead to bloating, acne, constipation, colds, food sensitivities, and more.

The easiest way to cut down on toxins is to make better choices about what goes in—and on—your body. If the air quality in your city isn't good, consider using an air purifier in your home. When you come in from the outdoors, leave your shoes by the door so you don't introduce allergens to your home. If your city's water supply is less than desirable, install a water filter or get a tabletop filter.

Bottled water isn't always better than tap water, and some bottled water *is* just bottled tap water. So, buy smart or use a filter. Drink plenty of clean, fresh water to assist the natural detoxification process.

Drink water. No news here. But, drink little sips throughout the day, especially two hours prior to a performance. It takes a while for your entire body to receive that hydration. Also, if you drink small sips during a practice session, you will ensure that your larynx is resetting in its neutral position, just in case you've been straining.

—COURTNEY COREY, FOUNDER AND DIRECTOR
OF THEATRE ARTS SCHOOL OF SAN DIEGO

Read the labels on your health and beauty products. If you wouldn't eat it, why put it in your hair or on your skin? Your skin is your largest organ. It absorbs everything you put on it and then it gets into your bloodstream. There are companies that specialize in all-natural, non-carcinogenic products. Find a brand you like and replace your deodorant, makeup, and other supplies with healthy varieties. Check the Environmental Working Group Skin Deep database at www.ewg.org for lists of options, and go to www.DebraWanger.com for more resources.

Work up a good sweat every day with cardio, hot yoga, or by going into an infrared sauna or dry sauna at your gym. Dry brush your skin to open your pores and release the toxins. If you need more detoxification, look into colonics or other cleansing methods and products. Decide for yourself how far you want or need to go with detoxification. I personally feel much healthier after cleansing and detoxification.

TAKE TIME IN NATURE

We used to spend time outside in nature, but most of us in modern society have built boxes around ourselves. We go from our apartment box to our car box to our theater box (or box office). We get little sunlight or fresh air or even touch the earth anymore. We force ourselves into contrived cycles of night and day. We ignore the sunrise and depend on alarms to tell us when to get up and turn off our electric lights when we want to sleep. Household appliances and outdoor power lines bombard us with electromagnetic pollution. In the theater and on movie sets, we're surrounded by unnatural lighting.

Offset the negative effects by spending time each day in nature. Get outside and feel the sunlight on your skin; take off your shoes and walk on the grass or sand—it's good for your hormones and your optic nerves. Being outside grounds all that electrical energy running through your body. Seeing the natural world—trees, flowers, oceans, and mountains—helps restore your natural cycles. Nature is calming and improves your mood. It's a great reset.

An actor's busy schedule makes it tough to schedule time in nature, so squeeze in "outside time" on the go. Skip the cab and walk. If you're taking public transportation, pass up the closest subway or bus stop and walk to the next one. When you're on a break from rehearsal—a five or ten—walk around the block.

Get some natural light on your skin. Vitamin D from the sun is good for you in moderation, so skip the sunscreen for just a few minutes. Go outside and soak it up. Ideally, just use a shirt or hat for coverage from the sun. Make getting outside part of your day, and schedule some time each week to get out in nature!

In some areas, the inside air quality is worse than the air outside. Use indoor plants to absorb chemicals and carbon dioxide (CO_2) or open a window and let the fresh air in. If you can't get out, look at pictures of nature in a book or poster, or on your computer. Just looking at nature can have positive effects on your well-being.

ENERGY MANAGEMENT ON A BUDGET

Maintaining your health and keeping your energy up can be expensive. You can spend a whole paycheck on food, supplements, and Spin classes, but you can stay healthy on a budget too.

I always carry easily portable snacks (nuts, carrots and hummus, apple and natural peanut butter, hardboiled egg) that are filling for in between work, class, workouts, auditions, and rehearsals!

—ADI MULLEN, ACTOR/DANCER, *SPRING AWAKENING*, CYGNET THEATRE; *FESTIVAL OF CHRISTMAS: NORTHERN LIGHTS*, LAMB'S PLAYERS THEATRE

BUDGET NUTRITION

Farmer's markets are a great place to pick up less expensive, high-quality produce. Look for the "ugly foods" that are misshapen but still good for a deeper discount. Make friends with the vendors at the farmer's markets and you could get an even better deal. A little charm can go a long way toward saving you money.

Organic fruits and vegetables can be pricey. Some fruits and vegetables are more prone to contamination from pesticides. If you eat the outside of the produce—like the skin of an apple—buy organic. If you peel off the skin—like the orange rind—buying organic isn't as important. Do an online search for the "dirty dozen" and "clean fifteen" of produce for lists of fruits and veggies that are most (and least) prone to pesticides, then decide for yourself which organic foods to buy and which non-organic foods are acceptable. Frozen vegetables might be your healthiest option, especially in winter.

Join up with friends to order foods in bulk and then split the cost. Costco has good prices on many bulk items. Online services like Amazon Subscribe & Save sell multipack and economy-sized foods and supplements; you'll pay less per pound or per item. Go online to find a ranch that sells grass-fed beef for a fraction of what you pay at the local supermarket or health food store. Some stores offer free shipping, so again, team up with friends to order in quantity. Meat is usually shipped frozen, so only order what your freezer will hold.

It's okay to buy food at the "dollar store," just make sure the food isn't older than you are. Read the labels to find foods equal to higher-priced items from the supermarket—and read the expiration dates.

Single-serving containers of foods like hummus or guacamole are a bit more expensive than buying in quantity, but they're still cheaper than fast food meals and snacks grabbed on the go. If you're going to be at an audition all day, pack a healthy, affordable, single-serving meal.

Eat In

Eat out less and start cooking at home. You can control the quality, portion size, and the cost of meals if you cook everything yourself. Restaurants add all kinds of chemicals, additives, sugar, and bad fats to make it taste so good.

Prepare meals in quantity and freeze the leftovers in batches so you can heat up a cheap, healthy, fast meal. I like to keep baggies of cut-up vegetables in the fridge so I can grab them on the way out the door. If you have a favorite salad from your local restaurant, try duplicating it at home to save money.

If you do eat out, avoid breakfast and brunch when the markups are highest. Eggs and toast are cheap, so make them at home and save your restaurant splurges for a nice dinner. Consider ordering just an appetizer and salad, or split an entrée with a friend.

Watch out for the beverage and dessert menus, which add a lot of cost to the tab for very little food in return. Beverages and dessert are usually unhealthy, too. The same goes for grabbing beverages on the go—those cups of coffee can add up in dollars and calories, too! Make your own coffee. I love my morning cup of Bulletproof coffee, which is made with grass-fed butter, MCT oil, and organic, toxin-free coffee. It replaces my breakfast with lots of yummy, healthy fats and keeps me full until lunch.

BUDGET EXERCISE

If you can't afford a gym membership or pricey home equipment, go online to find routines that use your body weight for resistance. Get outside and go for a walk in the park, the canyon, or along the seashore. You don't need expensive classes or activewear to get a good workout. Free or inexpensive exercise apps and YouTube come loaded with yoga poses and interval drills. You can do them on your schedule and with no special equipment. Perhaps work part-time front desk at a gym and get a free membership.

What skills do you have that you can use to barter for something you need? I used to trade voice lessons for private Pilates instruction. Can you give dance, singing, or acting lessons in exchange for a massage or other services? What about web design, yoga classes, hairstyling, or teaching knitting? Think about what you have to offer and how you can trade your skills for someone else's.

Physical touch from a partner is free, and something as simple as holding hands can make you feel good and relieve stress. You don't have to be rich to be healthy. Use your actor's imagination and design a plan that works for your head, your body, and your wallet.

BIO HACKS (IF YOU HAVE MONEY TO SPARE!)

Amazing technologies exist to hack your health and energy. There are hacks that promote meditation, relaxation, parasympathetic, and nervous system responses. Some hacks stimulate energy at the cellular level in mitochondria, the power plants in your cells. As quickly as I write these words on the page, the technology changes. New medical and technological advances use light, heat, cold, air, oxygen, pressure, and sound. These hacks can "shock" or work with your body, manipulate its systems, and accelerate natural hormone responses.

If you aren't on a tight budget and want to experiment, try any of the latest biohacks that promise to improve your body or your mind. Talk to your doctor first—and your banker—to see which ones are right for you. This is a fast-evolving field with new products hitting the market often, but here's a sampling of what's out there now.

COLD TREATMENTS

Cold thermogenesis, cold plunges, and ice baths can do wonders for mood, energy, and metabolism. There is a reason why professional athletes frequently use cold therapy for recovery. Cryotherapy chambers are popping up all over the place and give you a three-minute, invigorating blast. These experiences are energizing but can be dangerous if not monitored or done correctly. Use a reputable service that knows what risks to look for, how to protect you, and how to manage issues that may arise. Be smart and ease your way into it before trying ice baths so you don't get burned. For the free at-home version, try cold showers for a blast of energy.

FLOTATION AND SENSORY DEPRIVATION

Flotation and sensory deprivation tanks use large pods filled with water and Epsom salt, where you float in dark silence that's deeply relaxing and gives you a meditative break from the rest of the world. Some people have very transformative experiences during sensory deprivation. It's a great way to reboot and de-stress your nervous system. You can replicate some of this experience by soaking in a bathtub with warm water and Epsom salt.

Neurofeedback and high-tech meditation and relaxation devices can give you more control over how you think. You can change your brain waves and your thought patterns with cutting-edge technology. Seek out a trusted expert and see where it takes you.

BOUNCING AND VIBRATION

Bouncing on a mini-trampoline can stimulate your circulatory and lymphatic systems. The lymphatic system doesn't have a heart or other pump, so bouncing around on a trampoline wakes it up and helps "clean you out." Indoor trampolines are inexpensive and take up very little room.

A pricier option is a whole body vibration. Vibration plates were invented by NASA for astronauts who lost bone density due to time spent in space without gravity. Exercising on a vibration plate can stimulate your lymphatic circulation and give you a powerful workout. You have to balance and stabilize your muscles while you exercise on a vibration plate, so you also give your muscles an intense workout.

OXYGEN THERAPY AND RED LIGHT THERAPY

Hyperbaric oxygen therapy hyperoxygenates your cells in a pressurized chamber and can be very healing. It's used for disease management and anti-aging treatment, and some doctors' offices use these chambers for post-surgical recovery. Researchers are also exploring possible beneficial effects on everything from autism to cancer. Other oxygen therapies include EWOT (exercise with oxygen training), hypoxic training with special breathing training masks, and tricks to deprive, then flood you with oxygen during exercise. Again, work with a good trainer or doctor to get started with any of these.

With red light therapy, red LED lights can stimulate mito-chondria, the power plants of your cells. Infrared saunas can help you detox, speed up your metabolism, and make you feel great. Scientists are knee-deep in studying the healing effects of light on our bodies.

Monitors and wearables give you biofeedback to monitor your activity, breath, heart rate, and metabolism. Heart rate monitors and variability (HRV) training can teach you to vary your heart rate, which helps your parasympathetic nervous system. That means calming your ass down.

Smart drugs and nootropics may offer an array of supplements that can help you with mental focus, memory, and energy. Do your research, talk to your doctor, and proceed with caution. There are entire books on this subject, so if you want to go down that rabbit hole, know what you're getting into.

Genetic testing is an up-and-coming science that gives you information about your genetic tendencies, strengths, and weaknesses. That information can help you tune your diet, supplements, and exercise for healthier living. Get tested to see what you can do to improve your health and decrease your risk of disease. The cost of this type of testing is coming down from thousands to hundreds of dollars, and someday, genetic testing will be the norm. A less-expensive place to start is www.23andMe.com, although it has somewhat limited data at this point.

Liposomal supplements, cool sculpting, lasers, pressure, heat, and cold can be used for detox, mood, fat loss, and hormone regulation. Intrasonic Massagers such as Rapid

Release, and sound therapy like binaural beats, waves, and sonic resonance are emerging technologies in the health and wellness field. Stem cells from your fat or bone marrow introduced in an IV or re-injected in places of injury can heal and are also used to slow the aging process.

The list of biohack methods and technology is endless. Investigate the ones that interest you—and that you can afford—and give them a try. The speed at which this technology is changing is mind blowing.

FEED YOUR HEAD

Acting requires energy. Start with good nutrition, sleep, and exercise. Add supplements and biohacks as you need, and can afford them. Acting requires mental energy, too. While you're getting your body in shape, don't neglect the most important organ—your brain. A calm mind will give you strength and resilience to get through the challenges in your career.

Meditation is a powerful, easy, and free method for calming your mind. Meditation may be as simple as breathing exercises you do on the bus or subway, or it might be more structured, like tai chi or yoga class. You can sit quietly in a comfortable space in your home reserved for meditating. There are lots of good resources online to learn meditation if you are new to it. Sit still and prepare for the monkey mind. Practice the pauses between the thoughts, not expecting all thoughts to cease altogether. I'll get more into meditation in Scene 5.

Breathing is the most important tool for your brain. Slow, nasal breathing has a direct link to controlling your nervous system. Breathing through your nose changes the nitric oxide balance in your blood and gets you out of fight-or-flight—it communicates to our bodies that we are not in danger, and slows us down. Inhale essential oils to enhance the effects. Breathing is totally free—and it works!

You can also try massage, bubble baths, walking in nature, or talking to a life coach or therapist. All these activities can also calm your sympathetic nervous system—the system controls the fight-or-flight response you get when your body perceives something as a danger. You want to fight or defend yourself from the threat, but everything can feel like a threat. You might be in fight-or-flight mode all day long and not even realize it, then wonder why you're so tired at the end of the day.

Being in the moment and not thinking about the past or future—mindfulness—can have some of the same benefits as meditation. But rather than sitting motionless, you can be active during mindfulness. Cooking, exercise, playing the piano, and any activity that requires you to focus on the present can be relaxing for your mind. Mindfully focus on whatever activity you are doing and all the senses you are experiencing during it.

The saying "stay in your head and you're dead" refers to a tendency to overthink everything. Practice experiencing life with your senses and your heart. When you're stuck in your head, you're ruled by thought rather than feeling. You might see the world with an "us vs. them" mentality. The truth is, other people's actions are rarely malicious. They're usually just thinking about themselves, not trying to harm you. Take a moment to breathe into your heart, and see the world as being on your side and with your best intentions in mind.

Allow yourself to take breaks. We can only pay attention for so long. Take mini-breaks between all the focused, scheduled activities. There's a reason the Actors' Equity and Screen Actors Guild make you take regular breaks. Don't always sit down during these breaks—get up, move around, and get a change of scenery. Get out of the rehearsal room, or step away from your desk at your day job and do some jumping jacks or go for a walk. Laugh with a colleague.

Keep your brain active for optimal mental and cognitive performance. Read books, take a cooking class, or enroll in a college course. Many universities offer online classes and some of them are free. Brains love novelty. Challenge yourself to learn a new language or musical instrument. Develop a new skill that doesn't come naturally to you. Actors tend to stick to a single track—the acting track. Learning new skills and developing hidden talents will make your brain work harder, improve your memory, and keep your mind sharp. Use your latest acting project as a springboard for new research and learning.

We used to believe that our brains stopped growing and developing at a certain age. Now we know there's something called neuroplasticity that allows our brains to grow and learn as we age. There's a great book by Carol Dweck called *Mindset: The New Psychology of Success* that explores the power of a growth, rather than fixed mindset. Your brain is capable of growth and learning, so challenge it—and yourself—to grow and learn at every age.

Maintaining a healthy mindset can be challenging for an actor. Our schedules are erratic. We work at night when most people are relaxing, or on weekends and holidays when other people don't work at all. We have high demands on our bodies, our emotions, and our time. Those extra demands make self-care extra important. We ask a lot of ourselves with our work, and we need to swing the pendulum to the other extreme to stay balanced.

Acting is physically, mentally, and emotionally demanding but the rewards can be huge. The more resilience you bring to the profession, the greater the potential rewards. Promoting health from within will keep you in top form—most of the time.

WHAT TO DO WHEN YOU'RE SICK

I always remind my students that it's ok to be under the weather! If you can take the day off, do so. There's no medal to be won by playing through the pain. If you have a performance, try this on for size: consider that the character, today, may be a little sick. Don't try to hide the sniffles—work that into your reality. It's far easier to overcome feeling sick by accepting it than trying to pretend it's not happening. Audiences can see through that.

—ERIN CRONICAN, THE ACTORS' ENTERPRISE

Despite everything you do to stay healthy, you're going to get sick. Actors interact with people all the time. You're up close and personal with other actors. You're in each other's airspace, touching, hugging, and sometimes kissing. It's impossible to avoid the germs. Unfortunately, actors don't have the luxury of being sick. The show, as they say, must go on.

If you're lucky enough to have an understudy, someone might be able to fill in for you, but oftentimes, you're it. Do your best to avoid getting sick in the first place. Wash your hands often with soap and water and keep them away from your face. I use a probiotic spray instead of chemical sanitizer. You can also look into supplements like grapefruit seed extract, colloidal silver, and natural antibiotics. Also try essential oils like diluted oregano oil and Thieves oil to kill germs, support immune function, and prevent sickness.

Preventative care goes a long way toward keeping you from getting sick, but if you do get sick or feel like you're fighting something off, you'll have to do what's necessary to power through it. Drink plenty of water, get plenty of sleep, and take whatever medications you need to get better. I like Mucinex for getting rid of excess mucus, but simple steam can do wonders to clear your sinuses. Don't go out for drinks or spend time on exercising, which will wear you down even more. Take vitamins D, C, and zinc. Then do some detoxification, like infrared sauna, sweating, or floating in an Epsom salt bath to get all the junk out of your body. Sometimes just sleep is the best medicine for getting better. Take it easy with the exercise and get extra sleep.

HIDDEN ENERGY DRAINERS

Sleep and nutrition drainers zap your energy. Proper nutrition, restful sleep, and regular exercise fuel you. Those are the basics, but there's more. Hidden time suckers and bad habits also affect your energy. Be aware of activities that steal your energy and hold you back.

Do you have a habit of looking at Facebook or another social networking site, and the next thing you know four hours are gone and it's past your bedtime? Are there certain times of day when you're more likely to eat foods that aren't good for you? Are there situations where you're more likely to drink? Know what's bad for you and what triggers those behaviors and then do something about them. Set rules for yourself. No one else is going to do this for you, so you have to be an adult, make rules, and stick to them.

I love my castmates. They're awesome and fun to hang out with. But if I hang out with the cast after every show, I'm going to spend all my money, drink too much, gain weight, and feel like crap in the morning. Does that mean I have to avoid my cast? No, but I do have to limit how often I go out with them. Maybe my rule is to go out with them just once a week for two drinks, or twice a week and have one drink each time. Set rules for going out with your cast and for other activities like television and internet time. If these activities keep you up at night, set a limit on how much you watch or surf, and how late you do it. Through trial and error, see what works for your life and your habits.

What if you mess up, fall off the wagon and break a rule every now and then? Don't beat yourself up over it. Accept it, forgive yourself, and move on. Life is going to happen no matter how well we plan. There'll be days when you eat a doughnut, skip yoga class, or blow off your acting class. Stuff happens. Shoot for excellence and you'll still do well enough, even if you goof up every now and then. Sometimes, breaking the rules is totally worth it.

If you can't seem to get it together, remind yourself why you need to be at the top of your game. Why are you doing all this? Why did you choose to be an actor? Why do you want to be happy and healthy? You have reasons, and sometimes it helps to remind yourself of what those reasons are to stay motivated. If being an actor is important to you—if it's one of your life's priorities—you'll make rules for yourself and stick to them. Being an actor is *that* important to you. *You* should be that important to you.

WHAT CAN I DO TODAY?

Staying in tune is a lifelong process. Getting in tune starts with baby steps you can take today. The following three tasks will give you some fast, forward motion toward optimizing the big three—sleep, nutrition, and exercise—and set you up for greater health and energy.

- Head into the bedroom. This is where you (hopefully) spend one-third of your life. This is where you do that thing that's so important to your health and energy— sleep. Is this a good place for sleep? Is it dark and cool? Is it quiet? What can you do to make this a more restful place? Take an inventory and then make changes to this important place. Get rid of electronics you don't need and cover the lights on the ones that have to stay. Move your phone and charger to across the room. Do you need blackout curtains to keep out the light, a fan or white noise machine to drown out noises? Small changes to your sleeping place can improve your sleep and give you immediate results. You'll appreciate those changes the moment you wake from a good night's rest.

- Start a food diary. Write down what you eat and note how you feel later that day and the next couple of days. Are there foods that upset your stomach, make you break out, or make you jittery? Do some foods make you feel more energetic or focused? Eliminate foods that can create issues and see if you feel better. Replace your sugar with a natural sweetener like Stevia or monk fruit. Replace your wheat products with grains that are gluten-free. Add leafy, green vegetables to at least one meal every day. Look up the "dirty dozen" of produce and vow to buy organic when you can. Track your food and make sure you're getting enough protein, fat, and fiber. Then, make small changes and pay attention to how you feel. You might have immediate results as you opt for healthier choices, or it may be days or weeks before you notice a change. Stick with it and you *will* feel better.

- Do twenty minutes of exercise. You can do the full time

with cardio, strength training, or flexibility training, or you can mix it up and do seven minutes of each. Go for a run, do some squats, lunges, sit-ups, and push-ups, and reach over and touch your toes. Turn on the music and boogie.

Go do it.

Right now.

I'll wait right here for you. Twenty minutes.

INTERMISSION

Let's take a little break.

Take a breath.

Deep into your belly.

Smile and think about all you've done so far.

In Act I, "Find Your Ideal Balance," you set the stage for becoming a sane, healthy, resilient actor.

You imagined, visualized, and wrote your ideal life. You put your wishes, hopes, and dreams to paper. You considered your values, and asked yourself why you want what you want.

Your dream life includes the many pieces of your life.

Acting, health, family, and friends are all part of that balanced life that will give you the resilience you need to succeed in your profession.

You prioritized your dream life's goals and began a plan to achieve them.

You packed your audition bag and started taking care of business. You have new headshots and a resume, or a plan to get them. You're reading up on current productions and you may even have an audition scheduled.

You're also putting together the pieces of your health. You're looking at the status of your sleep, nutrition, and exercise and making positive changes.

Scenes 1, 2, 3, and 4 gave you simple tasks to put your plan into action. Did you do the tasks at the end of each scene? This is the best time to start.

Right now.

Those tasks will be easier now than later. They'll be much easier to do today than next week. If you start now, you'll be a week into your healthy, balanced life and career by this time next week.

Put this book down and go back to the "What Can I Do

Today" section at the end of each scene. Start at least one task from Scene 1, Scene 2, Scene 3, and Scene 4.

Come back when you're done. I'll wait here for you.

ACT II

MASTER THE BALANCE

You're building a solid platform for your life's stage. How will you master the balance on that stage? How will you pull all those pieces together into one beautiful, complete puzzle—your life's script?

In Act II, "Master the Balance," we'll explore the mentality behind the method to achieving resilience. We'll discuss how attitude, presence, and emotional intelligence affect you and your relationships. We'll also talk about dealing with stress and difficult people, both of which can throw you off balance.

Finally, we'll talk about how to get it all done. You're asking a lot of yourself and there's much to do. You'll have to dig deep. But this is your life, and you're worth it.

If theatre is your only thing going, you will go insane. Believe me. I am that person. I put all my eggs in one basket at times and I feel like I am a prisoner to it. It's easy to get depressed. I find myself binge-watching TV shows to take my mind off of it.

The waiting. It's terrible sometimes. Waiting for the next audition. Waiting to get that next job. I think going to the gym is a fantastic idea. It keeps your body in shape because you never know when you are going to dance at an audition.

If you can afford it, classes keep your mind working and your juices flowing. Classes are a definite help when it comes to the doldrums. It keeps you prepared while you wait...A lot of people do yoga. They swear by it. I also write. It keeps me creative while I'm not working.

—JOEL NEWSOME, *THE PRODUCERS, 42ND STREET,* BROADWAY; *CAGNEY,* OFF-BROADWAY; *BILLY ELLIOT, SOMETHING ROTTEN,* NATIONAL TOURS.

GET YOUR HEALTHY HEAD ON

For those who grew up with positive, healthy family experiences (who are they?), emotional health may come naturally. Many people didn't have that opportunity and carry childhood baggage into their adult lives. Acting can help to heal some of the trauma we accumulated as kids, but we can't rely on acting to fix us.

Regardless of where you fall on the emotional spectrum, there's often room for improvement. How we feel inside our heads and interact with others affects our happiness and our health. It also affects the opportunities that present themselves in our careers and their outcomes.

Getting your head straight is as important as your physical health. Just like good nutrition, sleep, and exercise, you have to work at it.

You can develop emotional health through self-help, but know when to ask for assistance from someone else. Even if we know *what* to do, it's often difficult to know *how* to do it—how to put all the concepts into action. If you're truly unhappy and doing it on your own isn't working, get professional help from a therapist or coach. Find out what's going on so you can move forward with your goals, your career, and your life.

PRESENCE

First, I love meditating because it not only helps ease my stress, but it also reminds me to stay present and grateful in what can be a cutthroat industry.

—ADI MULLEN, ACTOR/DANCER, *SPRING AWAKENING*, CYGNET THEATRE; *FESTIVAL OF CHRISTMAS: NORTHERN LIGHTS*, LAMB'S PLAYERS THEATRE

In acting classes, we learn to cultivate a sense of presence. It's that state when everything is fresh and new and happening for the first time. It's being in the moment. We want the audience to know we're 100 percent invested in that moment, that performance, and in them—those people who paid big bucks to spend time with us.

Developing the ability to be in the moment when you're off stage can be kind of a magic trick—but it's a trick you know how to do. You've done it and have seen the results on stage. You've been in that moment when the audience hangs on your every word. You've created that magic moment with your presence. Why not take your trick on the road and be present off stage too?

Every time our mind wanders to the future or the past, or to something that isn't right in front of us, we aren't being present. Being present takes practice. You aren't present when you're with someone and thinking about something or someone else. If they're talking and you're already thinking about your next response, you're not totally present. You're not tuned in to them or listening to their words. You're tuned in to yourself and your response. Presence is being in the moment, in the here and now, just as it happens.

BE WITH PEOPLE

Be with people—not with the grocery list or what you're going to say next. Let go of the horrible traffic you dealt with to see this person, because none of that matters at the moment. Care enough to give them your undivided attention. What matters is that you're that person's friend, coworker, actor, director, coach, lover. Maybe you just met them and they haven't figured out what your relationship might become. They'll be more open to finding out if you're interested enough to give them yourself in that moment.

Think about how it feels when you're speaking to someone who's distracted. You're giving them your time and you want to be their first priority, but they're not totally there. They're not present. They're waiting for you to stop talking so they can have their turn. Maybe they're even looking at their cell phone. Did they hear what you said? Did the words sink in? How does it feel when you interact with people like that? Do you feel empowered, or blown off? How do your friends feel when *you're* not present for them?

TRUST

Being present is about learning to trust. Have trust in the belief that what other people say is important enough for you to hear. Trust your brain to formulate an intelligent response when it's your turn to speak. Trust your mouth to say something appropriate at that time. You can do all that after the other person speaks and you've had another moment to digest their words. Instead of responding immediately, pause when they stop talking. Give them another moment. Maybe they have more to say. Present communication takes practice, but the payoff is tremendous.

Trust that your time together is more important than your phone. Trust that what you have to gain from the person speaking to you is more important than your email. Trust that looking that person in the eye and listening to their words is the best thing you can do at this moment in time.

UNPLUG

Your phone can be a huge distraction and make presence impossible. If you have alerts that notify you every time you get an email or social media update, turn them off. Even having your phone in sight can be a distraction, so put it away. Replace screen time with eye contact.

Practice presence at your next audition or rehearsal. Turn off your cell. Tuck it away. Talk to someone, then listen. Really listen to their words and think about what that person is saying. Listen more than you talk. Practice not cutting them off, interrupting them, or finishing their sentences. Practice *not* thinking of your next response while they're talking. Practice pausing after they stop talking. Savor that golden moment when no one's talking and see how they respond. *Now* it's your turn. Trust that you'll say the right thing, and you will.

DO LESS

One road to being present is choosing to do less. We tend to push ourselves to go, go, go and finish as many tasks as possible in the shortest time possible. We try to multitask, which isn't even possible. Multitasking is nothing more than switching back and forth between tasks really fast. It's not effective and doesn't allow us to give any of those tasks our full attention. We push ourselves to do too many things at once and expect people to respond to our accomplishments.

You might impress people with your accomplishments for a minute or two, but they'll remember how it felt to be with you—that's what sticks. Don't be so busy with tasks that you miss those moments with people. You could miss the best parts of your life.

A wonderful side effect of presence is becoming less afraid and more confident. If you think about it, fear is caused by worrying about the future based on experiences in the past. When you're in the moment and not thinking about the future or past, you have nothing to fear. Think about all those fears you have at an audition, rehearsal, or on stage.

What if I fall off the stage?

What if I forget my lines?

What if they hate me?

What if, what if, what if...all those what-ifs can turn the jitters into a self-fulfilling prophecy and increase the possibility of something bad actually happening. You can quiet them by being present.

BREATHE

How do you ignore all those past worries and future fears and focus on the present? Start with breathing. Take long, slow, deliberate breaths, and be aware of them and nothing else. Breathe through your nose. Relax your body, focus your breath, and let go of that fight-or-flight response. Listen to the sound of your breath and the sounds around you, and focus on each sense and be aware of what they are all telling you. What do you hear, smell, and taste? What do you feel? Tune in to your senses and become aware of everything you feel throughout the day. Look at your food, smell it and taste it as you put it in your mouth and experience every bite. If you feel your mind ruminating about past events or thinking about the future, bring it back to the present and what's going on around you. Do a quick reboot whenever you need it.

You can't be present every minute of every day, but with practice, you can get present quickly and often. You can learn to make yourself present at will and when it's most important. With practice, presence becomes more habitual and natural.

MEDITATE

I have discovered that yoga and meditation have been the most effective way to keep me sane as a working actor.

—ASHLEE ESPINOSA, REGIONAL THEATRE ACTOR AND ASSOCIATE
FACULTY OF THEATRE, RIVERSIDE CITY COLLEGE

Meditation is a great tool for developing presence. There's a reason meditation has been around forever: it works! Meditation trains you to slow down your thoughts, let go of accumulated stress, and be in the moment. It doesn't require any tools or tricks, and it's free.

Get in a comfortable position, close your eyes, and focus on your breathing. Take ten long, slow breaths, in and out, in and out. How do you feel? Isn't that nice?

Sit comfortably, breathe, and let go of thoughts and attachments to—or judgments on—thoughts. When thoughts do come up, notice them and let them float away. Don't expect your mind to completely shut off. Remember, if you're new to meditation, you'll probably get very antsy and have trouble quieting your mind. You can't eliminate all your thoughts (nor would you want to). But with practice, you can give yourself longer pauses and moments of peace between them. That's why you're doing it—to practice staying still, slowing down your thoughts, and letting go of the stress that your body racks up throughout the day.

With enough practice, you may have moments where you go into a deep, not-sure-where-I-went place, a deep theta brainwave state. Enjoy it, but don't expect it every time. Meditation is an opportunity for deep rest and to calm down your nervous system. Just show up and whatever happens, happens.

Slowly work up to meditating fifteen minutes twice a day. Ideally, meditate first thing in the morning to start your day off right, and again in the late afternoon, to recenter yourself. Find a place to meditate in your home, or do it on the bus or the subway on your way to work. I love to meditate in my dressing room after dinner break, between shows. Find a time and a place that works for you and make meditation a new habit, a gift you give to yourself every day. If you can't do it every day, the meditation police won't come after you, but you'll benefit from consistent practice. When we skip meditation, the stress starts to accumulate again. There are apps, classes, poses, and breathing exercises that facilitate meditation. If you need help, find what works for you and make meditating part of your daily routine.

UNLOAD

You may find it hard to meditate because your mind is cluttered with old baggage. Meditation will help to clear these out, but that lingering excess baggage needs to go so you can move on, unencumbered by the past.

Resilience requires doing your emotional homework. This means dealing with your demons. You may have people to forgive to reconcile your past. There are different methods for doing this: a friend, a journal, a therapist, forgiveness meditation. Nobody goes through life unscathed. Deal with the junk from your past so you can focus on the present. Do you need to forgive someone?

You could be harboring anger over something that happened a long time ago. Maybe you need to apologize for something you said or did, or maybe you need to confront someone over something *they* said or did. Forgiveness can replace that anger, resentment, or turmoil with calm, and it costs nothing to pick up the phone and have that conversation.

If you're worried about the outcome of those conversations, do it like an acting exercise and talk it out with yourself. Imagine the other person can hear you. Put them in an empty chair and "talk" to them. Or write them a letter and either don't send it or burn it. Just getting it out of your head and into the air or on paper can help. Get it out of the shadows and the dark spaces of your mind.

If you're struggling with past events, write about them, talk to yourself about them, or talk to a trusted friend, therapist, or coach. If you're always worried about the future, keep taking steps to move closer to your goals.

Action and progress will make the future less scary, so you can stop dwelling on it and be happy with where you are right now.

CHARISMA

Some people have an elusive quality that sets them apart from the rest of us. They radiate it. It's *charisma*.

Charisma is like presence on steroids. When Tom Cruise would stop by the talent agency, he radiated so much charisma I swear there were light beams coming out of him. His energy draws you in and you just want to bathe in that glow. I've never met Bill Clinton but I've heard he has the same effect on people. When you talk to him he makes you feel like you're the most important person in the world. He knows how to focus on a person and a situation and be totally present in the moment. That ability to focus on another human and let them know you're there for them—really there—is part of what creates charisma. That skill sets people like Tom Cruise and Bill Clinton apart from most of us.

There's a quote by the late poet Maya Angelou that sums up the power of charisma: "I've learned that people will forget what you said, people will forget what you did, but people will never forget how you made them feel."

Think about how *you* make people feel. Be present and

you will develop charisma and eliminate the thoughts plaguing you and the negativity that blocks that relationship. If you aren't focused on people, they'll sense it and remember how you made them feel in that moment. Make that moment about *them* and not about you.

The hardest part of paying attention to the people around you is remembering to do it. Cultivate your inner Bill Clinton, your Tom Cruise, and your Maya Angelou. Practice focusing on the people around you. When a director gives you—or someone next to you—notes, check into the moment and hear what he's saying. Practice with the people you don't know but see every day, like the security guard, the grocery clerk, and the cashier where you shop. Remember their name when you meet them. You'll have better experiences when you make the effort to engage with the people in your life. You might be amazed by how they respond.

Charisma is a huge asset in the acting business. Charisma can get you hired. If you're lucky enough to have been born with a charismatic personality, that's terrific! Make the most of it. If you're lacking charisma, all is not lost—you can develop more of it with practice.

AUTHENTICITY

Another piece of charisma is authenticity.

We all know people who aren't good looking in the traditional sense but are attractive because of their self-confidence. They're genuine and authentic. They're true to who they are. Likewise, we probably all know people we don't perceive as genuine. They're afraid to be themselves around us, so we don't trust them. They're a turnoff and we question their motives.

Authentic people are comfortable in their own skin. They are themselves—the best versions of themselves. As the playwright Oscar Wilde said, "Be yourself; everyone else is already taken."

Being the best version of yourself is better than being anyone else. We're all different, and that uniqueness is what makes us special. Like yourself and be that person. If you're not, people sense an incongruence with who you are and who you pretend to be. How you accept and treat yourself affects how you treat others. When you aren't true to yourself, you repel people, and that's the opposite of charisma. Be authentic.

On the professional side, no one is going to want to cast you in a show if they don't trust who you are. Remember, people invest time, money, and effort into a show and they need to know they can depend on everyone involved. If there's something about you that they don't trust—no matter how subtle—they'll move on to the next person.

They may not know why, but they'll sense something—that difference between who you are and who you're pretending to be. It's your authenticity and uniqueness that could get you the part.

As actors, we tend to look outside ourselves for validation and worth, but our true value lies within. Hold onto that power, that vision of who you truly are. Don't give that power away to someone else. They don't know you like *you* know you. Be true and be you. You're more than good enough.

EMBRACE YOUR FLAWS

Being authentic means embracing *all* of you—the good, the bad, and the flawed. Nobody expects you to be perfect. Perfection isn't even possible, so trying to achieve it is futile. People who appear perfect make us uncomfortable, and, if you appear too perfect, people won't respond positively to you. We all respond more favorably to some vulnerability.

It took me years to figure that out. I thought I had to be perfect in every aspect of my life. When I began to trust people to accept my shortcomings, my little imperfections and, well, my *humanness*, people really started to like me. We could connect because I was a real person then.

When I was trying to be perfect all the time I alienated people. Who wants to compete with or be around attempted perfection? I wasn't fooling anyone, of course. People see through falsification, and fakers appear haughty, conceited, obnoxious, or just plain out of touch. Everyone has flaws, scars, bumps, and bruises, physical or otherwise. Nobody gets through life unscathed. Being authentic includes being imperfect, so embrace your flaws and you'll be a happier person. Vulnerability and authenticity win.

Comparing yourself to others is never healthy. If you're comparing yourself to the "beautiful people," keep in mind that most of the perfect people you see on magazine covers are Photoshopped. They aren't perfect literally or metaphorically, and their lives aren't perfect. They're just as flawed as you and me, so resist the urge to compare yourself to them, and be happy with who you are. Work to make yourself better, but accept who you are at this moment. That means having a positive body image, even if you could lose a few pounds. It means knowing you're a good actor, even if you aren't currently in a show. It means knowing you're loveable, even if you don't currently have a girlfriend. It means having something to offer the world that's every bit as good as that famous actor or cover girl—because you do. Believe it.

EMOTIONAL INTELLIGENCE

You're smart. You have to be pretty intelligent to be a good actor. But are you emotionally intelligent? Unlike book-smart intelligence or IQ intelligence, emotional intelligence measures your ability to empathize with others. It's your capacity to understand how you impact them. It's about being self-aware and getting along with others.

Your emotional intelligence affects how you connect with people and your personal impact in social situations. It starts with being more present. Focusing on the problems of the past and future can prevent you from tuning in to your own emotions and noticing the emotions of the people around you. Being present will give you greater emotional intelligence. You can't pick up on non-verbal cues if you aren't paying attention.

As an actor, you have an advantage in the emotional intelligence department. You're trained to be aware of your body language and facial expressions and how people respond to them. You study other people's body language and expressions and try to figure out what they tell you.

Just as you can learn a lot by listening to your own body, you can understand other people by observing them. When you interact with people they may respond verbally, but they often say much more with their eyes, hands, or body language. Sometimes what they *don't* say can be telling. If you have trouble communicating with others, work on your emotional intelligence. The problem may be less about *what* you say and more about *how* you say it, or about how you perceive the response to your words.

Author and psychologist Daniel Goleman is an expert on the topic of emotional intelligence. If you want to learn more about developing your own emotional intelligence, I recommend you read his books.

THERE WILL BE STRESS

In terms of stress management, the first thing I help people to see is that we're all human, and this job is hurtful, disappointing, and anxiety-provoking. We need to remember that we feel these things because actors, by nature, are sensitive people. These feelings are not the problem. The problem is when we let these feelings change our self-worth. YOU ARE NOT YOUR DISAPPOINTMENTS. Give yourself a day to acknowledge and mourn the loss of a role or the stress of a project, and then move forward.

—ERIN CRONICAN, THE ACTORS' ENTERPRISE

Stress.

We may not understand exactly what stress is, but we all know what it feels like.

Anything that messes with your calm can cause stress. Maybe your dog's sick, you haven't worked for a week, or you're fighting with your boyfriend. Maybe you have to drive the 405—ever. Those situations can scramble your thoughts and feel like a fist around your heart, or a rock in the pit of your stomach.

I've gotten my stress more under control, but it wasn't always that way. When I worked at the Hollywood agency, the atmosphere was chaotic and we were always in crisis mode. Thinking, *Oh, my God. Donald Sutherland needs to get this script by this afternoon or the world is going to come to an end! You have to get this birthday present to Elizabeth Shue in Cairo by tomorrow!* That was the attitude, even though we all knew the script would go into a pile and the actor probably wouldn't read it for a week. We were in a constant state of fight-or-flight mode.

In those early days of the internet, you couldn't just directly email someone a script. You had to type up a cover letter, send the script and the letter to the copy room, and then run them down to the mail room. There was a lot of typing, running, and midnight drives to get documents to the right places on time. People yelled and threw things. Several movies came out around that time that showed the ugly side of Hollywood—intense, stressful, and full of mind f***s—and they were very close to the truth. I remember going to see *Swimming with Sharks*. People in the audience were laughing at the insanity, while I was thinking, *This isn't funny; it's true. Working in Hollywood can really be just like this!*

I said goodbye to that particular stress when I left the agency, but everyday stress still filters into my life and career. The stress I left behind was replaced by other stresses.

While it's a lovely fantasy, removing all the causes of stress in your life won't happen, especially if you're an actor. Your acting schedule is hectic and unpredictable. You may have a job in addition to acting. You're dealing with the business of the business, fine-tuning your instrument, and life in general.

Everybody—not just actors—deals with stress. It's a plague of our modern era. We rush from place to place and from one activity to the next, filled with negativity and fear. Stress can hijack your health and career if you let it. But you can make decisions every day to mitigate your stress.

SIMPLIFY

Stress can come from taking on too many tasks. Oftentimes, we spend so much time on tasks that don't matter, we don't have time for the important stuff. Then we feel stressed because our priorities aren't met.

Think about how much time you spend each day with "busywork" that doesn't improve your health and happiness or move you closer to your goals. Take a peek at your calendar, or keep a journal of how you spend your time for a week. You might be surprised at all the time wasters that fill your days and make you feel like you're always scrambling to get caught up. Simplify your life by doing fewer of the trivial tasks and focusing on what's really important. You may be using trivial tasks to avoid tackling the most important projects in your life. This is called procrastination. You can tell yourself that having an organized underwear drawer is important, and it will probably look fabulous, but it won't get you an audition.

CHOOSE HOW YOU RESPOND TO STRESS

One thing that creates stress is dwelling on how stressed you are. How many times has someone asked you how you are and you responded by telling them you're busy? Life isn't a busy contest, and no one's impressed if you're busier than they are. No one wants to hear how busy we are, and dwelling on our busyness can become a self-fulfilling prophecy.

I've expunged the following words from my vocabulary: busy, exhausted, stressed out, and overwhelmed. I was relying on those words instead of having real conversations. The more overwhelmed I claimed to be, the more overwhelming my life seemed. Yes, I have a lot on my plate on as an actor, coach, teacher, author, podcaster, and mom, but I'm in the driver's seat. I *can* choose to be less busy and less stressed. Now when someone asks me how I am, I tell them I'm great. And I ask them how *they're* doing.

Try it. The next time someone asks how you are, tell them life is pretty darned good. Ask them how their life is going. They won't recoil from your busyness. They'll lean into the fact that you're interested in their well-being. Try this: "I'm great, and so happy to see you. How have you been?"

STRESS AND YOUR HEALTH

Stress wreaks havoc on your immune system; so if you're stressed, you're more likely to get sick. In some careers, when you're stressed out you can take a sick day or a mental health day, but you can't be a stressed out, sick actor. On stage and on the set, people are looking at you and listening to you, and you can't hide—you have to perform. With high-definition television, everything shows. You need to be awake, alert, and at the top of your game. When you're stressed out and sick, you have low energy. You can't sing or speak well, and you could be unpleasant to be around. That will cause more stress, and then it takes longer to get healthy again. It's a cycle that you have to break or you'll never really be healthy.

When you're stressed, your body retaliates. Our bodies send us sensations of aches, pains, and other unpleasant messages when something's out of balance. Those messages start as whispers and become declarations, then roars. If you don't do something about those symptoms, you'll find yourself with more serious issues. Listen to your body and take steps to reduce stress before it becomes a bigger problem.

STRESS AND YOUR HEAD

It's hard to be present when you're stressed. In fact, stress is often the antithesis of presence. When you're stressed about something that's going to happen, you can't think about the moment. Your mind is someplace else. Stress can negatively affect your auditions and performances. Tension can tighten up your voice and body. It can cloud your thinking. You can't bring your A game or be charismatic or sexy if you're stressed.

You might think your stressed-out state of mind is a secret, but it isn't—stress is written all over your face, oozing out of your pores, and making the people around you uncomfortable. How do you feel around people who are stressed out? They have a frown where their smile should be and a furrowed brow—like an exclamation point—in the middle of their forehead. Their body and face are under so much tension that it seems they could explode at any moment. Stressed out people radiate a negative energy that's tough to be around.

STRESS AND YOUR CAREER

Would you hire someone who's exuding negative, stressed-out energy? Think about how one person's stress affects the rest of the cast and the show. Do you think the audience picks up on that tension? You bet they do. Being calm, relaxed, focused, and present will put people around you at ease. Reducing your stress can mean the difference between getting a part and not getting one.

Most of us have a lot going on in our lives and are under a lot of pressure, so telling us to relax isn't helpful. How do we calm down and separate ourselves from all that worry? How can we get from a state of stress to our relaxed, calm, happy place?

While you can't have a stress-free life, you can choose to avoid stressful situations. Allow yourself to say no to people and activities that may add to your stress. Give yourself a realistic amount of tasks to do on any given day. If you find yourself racing from one place to the next in a constant state of stress, schedule fewer appointments, then leave early for your appointments so you'll always be on time.

Bring something to read or something to do when you get

to your audition or rehearsal. Practice having a present conversation with another actor. Use that opportunity to work on your emotional intelligence and charisma skills. You'll lower your stress and you might even make a new friend.

You'll be better equipped to deal with the stressors in your life if you're already on the path toward a happier, healthier you. A nutritious diet, regular sleep, and exercise will make the stressful times bearable and you'll recover faster. Remove the physical stresses on your body. Regular meditation will give your mind a calmer baseline so you won't be as easily affected by issues that cause stress. Get out in nature. Take yoga. Float. You won't eliminate all stress, but you can manage it.

YOU'VE GOT TO HAVE FRIENDS

Friends. My god. You must have a network of shoulders to cry upon. Friends are the most important thing of all.

—JOEL NEWSOME, *THE PRODUCERS*, *42ND STREET*, BROADWAY; *CAGNEY*, OFF-BROADWAY; *BILLY ELLIOT*, *SOMETHING ROTTEN*, NATIONAL TOURS

There was a time in my past when friendships were the lowest priority in my life, far below my children, career, and everything else. That was a very lonely place for me. I still need to give myself reminders to reach out to my peeps and not try to do it all by myself.

In cave times, we wouldn't have survived without our tribe. We needed each other to slay the saber-toothed tiger or kill the buffalo for lunch. We also needed touches, kisses, hugs, conversation, sex, and a way to perpetuate our species. While we've moved out of caves and don't have to worry about tigers and buffalo, we still need people. We're social creatures and being part of a group is important to our happiness. Developing deep, social connections may not save your life, but it can have a powerful impact on your health, balance, and resilience.

IT'S OKAY TO BE PICKY

The people you hang out with most often have the most influence on you, and you become more like them. Like author Jim Rohn once said, "You are the average of the five people you spend the most time with." Who's in your fab five?

You can lower your stress by being selective about your personal relationships. Choose happy, calm people to be around. We tend to pick up the habits—positive and negative—of those around us. Positive people will lift you up and negative people will bring you down. My closest friends have good attitudes, take care of themselves, and encourage me to do well and be well. It's no accident that those are the people I choose to spend my time with!

Are there people in your life who drain you? Energy vampires who are always negative, always complaining, and who bring you down? People who "suck all the air out of the room?" Or are there people you've simply outgrown—people you no longer have anything in common with and don't share any of their interests or values? If you aren't getting anything positive out of these relationships, then decrease the time you spend with those people or phase them out of your life. You aren't obligated to maintain every past relationship, and if people are sucking the life out of you, relegate them to Facebook friend only and share your real face time with people who support you and make you feel good.

LOOK BEYOND YOUR CAST

It's natural for all our activities to revolve around acting, but there's more to your life than being an actor. Make friends with people who aren't involved in film or theater. Meet people who aren't entertainers. You need other people in your life to help you become well-rounded and experience life outside of acting.

Make connections outside your comfortable group of actor friends. Join a Meetup group so you'll have scheduled times to meet with people who share your other interests. Go out in the daylight when most of your theater friends are asleep. Hang out with chefs, teachers, runners, hula-hoopers, triathletes, or whatever it is you have in common with other people. You can still love acting, actors, film, the theater, and everything about your acting life—just don't spend all your social time with actors and only talk about acting.

The added benefit to cultivating a varied circle of friends is that you'll be appreciated for more than your acting skills and become less reliant on them for your self-worth. You'll begin to see your total value. Eggs. Basket. You can do the math.

MAKE THE FIRST MOVE

Our actor friends tend to fade into the background when a film wraps or a show closes. Keep in touch with your performer friends between shows. Facebook is great for touching base, but don't rely solely on social media to maintain friendships. Get out and see people face-to-face. Invite them someplace—don't rely on them to invite you.

Don't become so busy that you isolate yourself. Spend quality time with those people who are good for you and help you become a better person. Cultivate those relationships, and if there aren't any people in your life like that, then seek them out.

TOUCH

Touch is a basic human need that feels good, and we often don't get enough of it. Hug people when it's appropriate or just shake their hand. Get a massage. Touch is magic. Think about it and make it count. It may be the only contact you have all day and it may be the only contact the other person has with another human being all day. Human contact is free, easy, and powerful.

REST AND RECOVERY

There's a natural cycle to work that includes rest and recovery. Without it, you'll burn out. All cycles of life include rest and recovery. There's emotional burnout, physical burnout, creative burnout, psychic burnout, and burnout from doing too many crappy, non-rewarding roles. Taking care of yourself will protect you from burnout.

We aren't built to work, work, work, with no breaks. Actors' Equity Association and SAG-AFTRA require producers to give us breaks for a reason.

Listen to your body when it starts to whisper that it needs a break or playtime to counteract the work. Recharge with whatever nurtures you. Take a warm bath, get a massage, go for a walk, or read a pulpy novel—whatever brings you to your balanced place. Sometimes I play my harp, sit in the sauna, or call my mom to recharge. What is it that makes you lose track of time and not think about the past or the future, and brings you into the present? Make time for those things when you need to recharge.

We do much of our work on our own time—looking for auditions, preparing for roles, studying lines—so it's easy to forget to take a break. Allow yourself time throughout the day to call a friend, get your nails done, hit the gym, or sip a cup of tea. Step outside and breathe in some air, or take the dog for a walk (he needs it too!) and come back refreshed.

Weekly recovery periods are important, too. Find something that really helps you recover physically, mentally, and emotionally. For me, getting into a float tank does the trick. Sensory deprivation gives me a full-body, deep relaxation and puts me in a meditative state. During that time, I go to another level of rest and clear my mind. My kids aren't needing me, my students aren't needing me, my clients aren't needing me, and my to-do list isn't calling my name. I can let go and give myself a break to rest and recover.

Take a day off from your cardio and weight-training workouts and do something restful. Yoga, tai chi, and other gentle body movements can help you relax. You can do them on your own at home with an online video or DVD. Better yet, take a class so you can connect with other people who enjoy yoga or tai chi.

Schedule some extended time off for yourself if possible. Take a vacation every few months or at least once a year. You're not going to magically find a free week on your calendar unless you put one there, so schedule it, plan it, and go! Do your best with your actor's feast-or-famine schedule.

Many people find rest and recovery through prayer or by reading inspirational material, going to church or synagogue, or by meeting with a spiritual group of their choice. Other people prefer 12-step meetings to recharge. If this resonates with you, find a faith-based group that meets your beliefs and devote time every week away from the intensity of work.

WHAT CAN I DO TODAY?

Start getting your healthy head on with mindful techniques like presence and meditation—anyone can learn them! You can practice them anytime, anywhere, and best of all—they're free! Then add someone new to your life. Make a friend.

- Practice presence in your next conversation. Go to the bank, grocery store, or coffee shop and practice with the stranger behind the counter—ask them how they're doing and listen to their response. They're human, just like you, and have just as much going on in their lives as you do. Put yourself aside, be interested in what they have to say, and be present for them. Make every conversation a present interaction and notice how people respond to you.

- Find a quiet place in your home to meditate. Go there now, make yourself comfortable, close your eyes and clear your mind. Take ten slow, deep breaths—breathe *innnnn*, breathe *ooooout*, breathe *innnnn*, breathe *ooooout*—and imagine all the stress leaving your mind and body. Stay there (for five minutes if you're new to meditation, or fifteen if you're more experienced) even if you get antsy or monkey mind. I'll be here when you get back. How did it feel to let go of all that stress? Make meditation part of your daily routine and practice it whenever and wherever you need it.
- Aside from acting, what do you like to do? What are your *other* interests? Think about what else you like to do, read about, and talk about. Make a list and pick at least one other interest to pursue. How will you learn more about this interest? Will you research it online, get a book and read about it, or join a group of people with the same interest? Find people who share your interest and develop at least one new friendship outside your acting life.

SCENE 6

MANAGE YOUR MINDSET

My favorite piece of advice about mindset [and] the business is, "If you're right for the role you can't do anything wrong, and if you're wrong for the role you can't do anything right." The secret is that you're not in control of either of those things, so you go in and do work you're proud of, and let them work out the rest. It leads to a much more empowered actor.

—ERIN CRONICAN, THE ACTORS' ENTERPRISE

You're a professional. You arrive at every audition and rehearsal a few minutes early, well rested, and prepared. But what's going on in your head? What you're thinking will affect how you look and behave.

Our brains generate thousands of random thoughts. Like TV commercials that interrupt our shows, most of them are distractions. Just as we filter out all that chatter on television with DVRs and the fast-forward button, we can skip past thoughts that clutter our minds.

Cleaning up the mental garbage takes conscious effort. When you start to dwell on useless or negative thoughts, replace them with something else. Affirmations make better commercials, and so does bringing your mind back to the present. If you need help, enlist technology. You probably set alarms and reminders on your phone that tell you when to get up or when you have an appointment. I like to set daily reminders to think positive thoughts, to stop thinking and meditate, or to take five deep breaths. Plug positive affirmations into your phone to remind yourself that you're an awesome human being, a great singer, or a wonderful girlfriend; then, use those thoughts to override the negative ones your brain is perpetrating.

You don't have to linger on negative thoughts your brain constantly feeds you. It's your brain—take control of it.

MENTAL GARBAGE AND NUTRITION

Be mindful of what you put into your head all day, and be selective about what you let in. If you're in the habit of setting the car radio to aggressive music, negative talk radio, or the traffic report, find a new radio station. Listen to an audiobook with a great story, or an inspirational podcast to offset all the negativity that seeps in throughout the day. All that noise, traffic, and bad news can bring you down without you even being aware of it. You control the food that goes into your body and you can control your mental nutrition too.

Watching violence on television can have a negative impact on how you feel. Some of my clients stopped watching the evening news because they found that most of it was so negative that it disrupted their mindset. You don't need to insulate yourself from what's going on in the world, but be mindful of how much time you spend exposed to stressful information.

For some people, even horror movies can have a stressful effect on their mindset. Think about what those images are doing to you. If they're messing with your head, make the decision to create a more uplifting and positive environment for your mind. Be especially aware of what you watch before bed. Your brain and body are the basis for everything else when it comes to leading a balanced life. Being good at anything—a good actor, employee, friend, father, or wife—will be easier for you if your body and your mind are in a healthy place.

YOUR POSITIVE ATTITUDE

Negative thoughts are like weeds. If we leave them unattended, they take over. Be aware of the negative things you say to yourself and flip them around. You might have a voice in your head saying, *I'm so fat that no one is ever going to love me.* Come up with an affirmation to bury that awful thought. It may not be, "I'm a tall, slender model," but it could be, "I'm healthy and beautiful. I'm committed to loving and appreciating my body every day. I'm worthy of love." Find the positive and focus on love and acceptance.

SUCCESS RITUALS

You can ease your nerves by developing routines or rituals. These are especially effective for auditioning. The key is to work out a predictable set of thoughts or actions that put you in the right mindset. Part of your ritual may be voice warm-ups or meditation. Breathing exercises with slow, deep, intentional breaths are wonderful for calming nerves. When thoughts take us out of our body, intentional breathing brings us back in. You can listen to a song that gets you pumped up, do some relaxing moves like yoga or tai chi, or read a passage from a favorite book. Maybe there's a smell that makes you feel just right, like lavender or lemon essential oil. Try different rituals until you figure out what puts you in the zone for auditioning. You can tinker with the recipe until you find that perfect mix.

Some people are superstitious and have routines that may seem odd, but they work. You may have a lucky shirt, or a catch phrase that you say to someone or to yourself just before you audition. It doesn't have to make sense if it works. It's the routine and predictability that makes you calm and confident.

Breathe, smile, and move your body to reinforce the state you want to be in. That calm, confident you is the first impression the casting director has of you. Breathe, smile, move, and carry that calm mindset through the whole audition.

HYPNOSIS AND TAPPING

Hypnosis is a great tool for rewriting that script in our heads. You can work with a professional hypnotist, download or purchase recorded material to listen to, or record your own voice and listen to the new dialogue that you're going to have with yourself.

Emotional Freedom Technique (EFT), or "tapping," is another method you can try. It utilizes affirmations and positive statements while tapping on specific meridians that coordinate with acupressure and acupuncture points. Tapping has been used to treat people with trauma and phobias. I use it when I'm stressed out before an audition or during a really bumpy plane flight to help calm my nerves and drive out negative thoughts. There are practitioners who can teach you about tapping or you can teach yourself how to do it. I like it because it's free, easy to learn, and you can do it anywhere or anytime. The Tapping Solution website is a good resource to learn more about EFT.

POWER POSES

Power poses can also put you in a more positive state of mind. Athletes naturally go into power poses after they win a race or a game, raising their arms in an outstretched "V" or putting their hands on their hips like Wonder Woman. Amy Cuddy talks about power poses in her book *Presence* and she has a TED talk that you can view online. Standing in a power pose for a couple of minutes can have a dramatic effect on how you feel. I do power poses as part of my morning routine and have incorporated them into my rituals before an audition or a show. There are several poses that work—learn them, use them, and see if they work for you. Tap into your inner Wonder Woman. It's empowering *and* it's free!

If you're somewhere where you can't do a power pose, at least have good posture. It starts with your physicality. When you're depressed, you tend to slump forward and keep your head down. Pull your shoulders back and stand up straight. It'll make you look confident; but, even more importantly, you'll *feel* confident. You know, act the part.

Get into that positive mindset before every audition or

performance and visualize how you're going to present yourself. Actually *picture* yourself walking into the room. Are you standing up straight and tall? Are you smiling? Did you make eye contact with people and greet them, make them know that you're happy to be there? Did you connect with the people in that room? Were you warm and friendly? Imagine yourself centered, relaxed, and ready. Visualize it, clearly imagine how it will feel, and then make it happen.

DEALING WITH DIFFICULT PEOPLE

Everyone has their own perspective on life. People who see the world in a positive light—and see all the good things in you—will make you feel more positive. If you need support, reach out to people who lift you up and be there for them too. If you need help learning your lines, call one of your upbeat friends to work on lines with you.

Some people have an unhealthy, negative outlook. You have to interact with many types of people, so how do you keep a positive mindset when you're around negative people?

The acting profession has its share of negativity. People who always complain and focus on what's wrong with the world will bring you down with them. It's easy to be sarcastic standing in the wings, sitting in the makeup trailer, or at the bar after the show. That complaining can drive you down. When you're tempted to say something negative, pause for a moment and think of something positive to say instead. Resist the temptation to join in on gossip. You never know who's listening, whose feelings you might hurt, or if you'll be the next target of that gossip! Be a role model of kindness to others and it will come back to you.

Humility is an attractive trait, so be humble and avoid name-dropping. Directors can read your bio or resume, and other actors can get to know you and make up their own minds about you. You don't have to push it to prove yourself to people. In an interview with Charlie Rose, actor Steve Martin's advice to aspiring performers was, "Be so good they can't ignore you." Be as good as you can be in your profession and don't worry so much about how everyone else is doing. Don't compare yourself to them, or be quick to judge them. Just be good—very, *very*, good.

If there are people in your show or on the set who are always negative and gossipy, avoid them. You don't have to be confrontational, but you don't have to hang out with them either. Keep in mind that most people want to be liked and they pick up on social cues. If they don't, tell them you aren't comfortable listening to the negativity and gossip. Tell them you're working on your positive attitude and they're welcome to work on it with you. See how they respond.

MIND F***S

There are producers and directors out there who are absolute jerks, and sometimes you have to work with them. They're unhappy and they enjoy making everyone around them unhappy.

Be professional and don't take their attitudes personally. If they're really awful, don't work with them again. If you're working on your health, happiness, and resilience, you can deal with awful people and not let it get under your skin. Don't take it personally. If the situation gets to the point where you can't or simply don't want to deal with them anymore, then quit. You deserve better.

Life is too short to waste on miserable, unhappy people, so don't give them another minute of your time.

ABUNDANCE MENTALITY

We tend to take for granted how easy our lives are. Compared to many people in the world who suffer in unsafe and unhealthy environments, we're incredibly lucky. Yet, with all our good fortune, we tend to focus on those things that we don't have. We can change our focus on that imagined scarcity of resources and cultivate an abundance mentality by expressing gratitude.

Many people keep a gratitude list—things they're grateful for today. What's wonderful about this day? There's always something in our lives to be grateful for; but, if we don't ask ourselves that question and write down the answer, we may never be aware of it. Being grateful out loud and listing some of the things you're grateful for are good exercises to practice with your spouse or your kids each night.

Practice developing an abundance mentality during times when you're most likely to worry about not getting what you want. Shift the focus from what you *might not* get to what you *will* get. On the way to an audition, ask yourself, "What's going to be great about this audition?" It's going to be fun, you'll see people you know and meet some cool, new people. What else could happen that'll make the audition great? Ask yourself that question and then answer it. Go with positive what-ifs.

Before you walk into the audition, think about how grateful you are for the opportunity to be there. Tell a friend at the audition how grateful you are to be there. Say things like,

- Isn't it great to audition for this show?
- We get to perform in front of an audience and get feedback.

- We might get a part, but if we don't, that's okay because someone else will get it.
- If we don't get a part, there's another part out there for me and for you.

That abundance mentality is a mental shift from our typical attitude and the desperate belief that we *have* to get a part. Why? Is this the last play, the last film, the last commercial, the last audition, ever? Of course it isn't, and it *may* be our part, but it may *not* be. So what? There's plenty for everyone and we'll get the part that's right for us.

The Buddhist philosophy of detachment from an outcome suggests we divert our focus away from the desired outcome of our work and focus on the work itself. That can be difficult, considering how goal-oriented most of us are. The secret lies in putting forth the effort and doing all the preparation, the homework, and the actual *work* required to achieve your goals. Do the work. Then release your desired outcome in the universe. Let go of it and trust the universe to respond.

LOOK AT YOU

Imagine two versions of yourself. One is desperate for a role and focused on the outcome of the audition. The other version of you is prepared, confident, relaxed, and thrilled to be auditioning because that's your main goal—

to audition—so you know you're going to succeed. Which version of you is going to give the best performance, and who is the director more likely to hire?

When you focus less on the outcome and more on giving it your personal best, you'll rarely be disappointed. Whether you get the part or not, you can walk away knowing you nailed it, and that's a major accomplishment. It's the only part of the audition you can control, so wracking your brain trying to figure out why someone made the decision they did—whether or not to cast you—accomplishes nothing.

Be the best, truest, purest version of yourself and trust the rest. Good things will happen—believe it! Whatever happens, you won't be disappointed because you freed yourself from expectations. You'll always have something—more knowledge, new connections, improved skills—to show for your hard work.

There's a misconception that we should strive to be happy all the time. But bad things happen, and the feelings they cause are appropriate. Our goal is, when things that challenge our happiness happen, to be able to bounce back from them. Accept the bad with the good and develop the resilience to move on. If you're angry or sad, own it. Say, "I feel angry." It's normal to feel every emotion, including the uncomfortable ones. When we resist them, it makes them worse. You can keep *always feeling happy* off your "should list." Be angry, be sad, be impatient, or be disappointed. Allow yourself to feel that emotion, just don't wallow in it. Accept it and then keep going. Bounce back, you resilient actor, you!

WHAT CAN I DO TODAY?

Managing your mindset often boils down to filtering out negative thoughts and replacing them with positivity, trust, and gratitude.

- Are there certain times of day when you feel anxious or depressed? Maybe your mindset changes after watching the morning news or after you sit in traffic. Could you skip the news and take a different route to work? Write down one time of day when you're at your lowest. Think of what you can do to change it. If you can't avoid whatever triggers your mood, think of how you might offset it with positive mental nutrition. If you *have* to take that route to work, maybe you can enjoy an audiobook on the way.
- Who are the most difficult people in your life? Make a list. Hopefully, it's a short one! Brainstorm ideas for dealing with these people. Come up with at least one way to decrease your time spent with each of them. If you can't avoid them, figure out how you're going to manage the next conversation with them. Write yourself a script and practice it.

• What's pretty awesome in your life right now? Do you have a cool apartment? Are you in a good relationship? Do you have a fantastic smile? Is the rent paid and the refrigerator full? What do you have to be grateful for? Make a gratitude list of ten things in your life that are wonderful. Make it longer if you like! Write them down and read your list out loud:

  · I'm grateful for my dog!
  · I love my smile!
  · I paid rent!
  · I just finished another chapter of this book!

SCENE 7

G.S.D. (GETTING S**T DONE)

Actors play many real-life roles on and off stage. Each role comes with responsibilities. Think of those responsibilities as juggler's balls.

For our actor role, we have to maintain our appearance and work on our technical skills—that's a couple of big balls. For our business role, we keep our resumes and headshots up-to-date, market ourselves, look for castings, network, book jobs, and audition. Another role and many more balls.

In our self-care role, we manage our nutrition, sleep, manage stress, and exercise. One, two, three more balls. We also have personal lives—family, friends, and fun— where we play many roles, and each one comes with balls of responsibility. Many of us have second and even third jobs. More roles, more responsibilities, and more balls. (Insert your own joke about balls here. Enjoy).

That's a lot of balls to juggle and a lot of roles to play. Fortunately, actors are natural at playing roles. We aren't naturally organized, but we can learn to be organized and keep all those balls from hitting the floor.

OFF STAGE, YOU'RE THE DIRECTOR

The truth is, everyone's brain works differently and no one system works for everything. But one thing is true: having NO system is a problem for everyone! I'd recommend thinking about a time in your life when things felt effortless and clear—see if you can mimic those conditions and create a system of organization that works for you.

—ERIN CRONICAN, THE ACTORS' ENTERPRISE

When you're in a show, you have a stage manager and a schedule with call times and rehearsal times. When you're on set, you have a call sheet and assistant directors who tell you where to go. You know where you're supposed to be, when you're supposed to be there, and what you're supposed to do when you get there.

On set and on stage, your time is organized, but your personal time may not be organized at all. You need to wrangle all that time between shows or on set when you need to be working on your craft and on yourself, and doing the tough part—getting work.

Acting isn't like an office job where you show up at 8 a.m., take lunch at noon, head home at 5 p.m., and then have the evening to yourself. Actors don't work Monday through Friday and get weekends off. They don't get two weeks of vacation every year, and they can't count on getting time off for the holidays. Actors don't have the same constraints on their time that people in other careers have—which is a blessing and one of the perks of being an actor—but that freedom can be a curse. As an actor, you have to learn how to manage your time to be productive.

Many of us have non-acting day jobs to supplement our incomes because, let's face it—it's a challenge to earn a living as an actor. If you live in New York, L.A., or another acting hub, your cost of living is higher than it would be in other parts of the country too. It isn't fair, but that's how it is. That other job takes up a lot of your time, leaving even less time for getting your acting career together.

There's a reason I put all that good stuff about taking care of your body and your mind in the first part of this book. If you aren't healthy, you can't be productive. You have to eat well, exercise, and get enough sleep to show up and be your best as an actor. If you don't, you may be able to work for a while or in short spurts, but to bring your A game every day and have a long-lasting, sustainable career, you need to be in good shape physically, mentally, and emotionally.

I know it's hard. You have my sympathy and understanding, but you need to get organized to be productive.

BE YOUR OWN BOSS

When it comes to managing my time, I can't just wing it. I need a written plan of what I'm going to do and when I'm going to do it.

You know how your producer and director manage your time on the stage or set? When you aren't working on a show you have to be your own boss. Be demanding, but be fair too. If your director allowed you to slack off all the time, the show would flop. It's the same with how you manage your own time. If you don't have a plan and stick to it, your own show—your *life*—is going to fall flat.

You can use a workbook, an online calendar, a notebook, a spreadsheet, or a scheduling program, but choose a system that's easy and accessible or you won't use it. If you're visually oriented, use colored pens, highlighters, and stickers to brighten up your workbook. You can color-code activities on your online schedule. *The Resilient*

Actors' Workbook is specifically designed to guide you through all these processes.

First, block out all the times that are non-negotiable: a day job, classes, rehearsals, shows, and anything else that's already scheduled for a specific day and time. Choose colors for each category and color-code them; this will allow you to see the different aspects of your life at a glance. Now look for blocks of time where you can add in all those other things you need to do to support your health and your career.

The goal is to create a balance between career, family, friends, health, and leisure time. Balance does not mean equal time, but as much time as is needed to give each their due. Be honest with yourself about how much time that rehearsal will really take, and include travel time. If you over-schedule yourself, you'll be rushing from one activity to the next all day and you'll burn out fast.

Having a plan decreases your odds of getting sucked into snacking, television, or Instagram, because you'll have something else to do. Those tasks, activities, and events should move you closer to your health, happiness, and career goals. Your schedule should reflect the goals you set for yourself, goals that satisfy your *whys* and all those things you're passionate about that will bring you closer to that life you imagined.

It takes self-discipline to stay on task when there's no boss breathing down your neck, but that's a skill you have to develop as an adult who's chosen this career. Lay out your calendar and see if it makes sense for you.

I like to put aside an hour to look over my whole week and see if I have enough time dedicated to my health, working on my career, and all my other priorities. It's easier to achieve balance over a week than trying to devote time to everything every day. I make sure that I'm covering all my bases and spending enough time on each activity to make steady progress toward my goals. If I have a goal to book two shows before the end of the year, I need to ask myself if I'm scheduling all the tasks necessary to make that happen. Am I checking the trades every week? Is my resume up to date? When's the last time I met with my agent? Did I block out time to work on audition material?

Look over your whole month, and each week, and see if you're spending enough time on all those things that are important. We all need a breather, so ensure you have enough downtime, too, so you can stay balanced.

DRESS YOUR SET

Your physical environment affects your productivity. If you spend time every day looking for your keys or your favorite yoga headband, you'll waste time and have less time to be productive. Being disorganized will make you late to appointments and you'll likely be stressed out and unprepared when you get there.

Decluttering your living space can be a challenge because everything you own has a story attached to it. Let's say you have a souvenir, like a seashell from a vacation. Every time you look at it, you're reminded of the beach and how calm and wonderful that was—you want to remember that. But you might also have a picture of an old boyfriend laying around that haunts you, or half-done projects that need to be finished (like a package that needs to be mailed), or a basket of laundry that needs to be folded. You have to leave those things out or you'll never do them, right?

Those objects all talk to you; they make noise. If they drag you down, make you feel bad, or remind you of an unhappy time, do something about them. You may think you've trained yourself to not see all that clutter, but your brain sees it. You know it's there, consciously or subconsciously, and it's dragging you down. Clean it up. Finish those projects or get rid of them.

I attempt to have a place for everything and put everything in its place. If I keep my keys in the same place, I can grab them on the way out the door so I'm not late to rehearsal or to an audition. If your apartment's a cluttered mess, your brain's going to feel cluttered. A clean, calm, relaxing environment promotes productivity and peace.

Some great books have been written that'll step you through the *hows* and *whys* of getting organized. I like Marie Kondo's *The Life-Changing Magic of Tidying Up* and Julie Morgenstern's *Organizing from the Inside Out*. The gist is, you should only keep things in your environment that make you feel great or serve a purpose. You have to be willing to let things go.

Imagine your hero is coming over. Do you want Stephen Sondheim or Steven Spielberg to see your place like it is right now? Are you proud of that place? How well does it represent you? Is it calm, confident, and put together, or is it a scattered mess?

Part of the decluttering process is putting the brakes on shopping. If you see something you like, put it on a list or add it to your Amazon Wish List or online shopping cart—don't check out just yet. Give yourself some time and distance to decide if that thing you're spending your hard-earned cash on is something you need or an impulse buy. It's easy to convince yourself that you need to buy something because it's on sale, or it's cute, but do you need it? If you bought everything that was cute or on sale you'd have a house full of stuff you don't need. And some of us do.

We all tend to buy much more than we need. If we focused on buying less and getting rid of what doesn't really rock our world, imagine how much more space (and cash) we'd have. Be the boss of your space. Make it reflect your best self: clean, uncluttered, filled with things you love, and organized for productivity and success.

DEALING WITH A SCHEDULE THAT'S ALWAYS CHANGING

Your calendar is looking good! Everything you need to do is scheduled—with times, dates and places—and you even color-coded it. You're in for a ridiculously productive week!

Are you really going to be super productive? You need to be flexible, too, because actors' schedules are always changing and so is life. The rehearsal call time is going to change, your car is going to get a flat tire, your cat is going to get sick, and you're going to get a callback. All those things will happen and they could all happen on the same day.

Be flexible and understand that a great schedule you can't fully meet is better than no schedule at all. You'll still get some things done, and you can't beat yourself up over what you can't accomplish. Remember to leave some light, unscheduled buffer time to absorb some of those last minute delays or adjustments. Smile and be happy for what you did, then deal with the changes.

HAVE A B-DAY

This isn't about your birthday (although if it *is* your birthday, happy birthday).

Your acting career will be different from day to day or week to week. Plan for variations with different routines. You may have a routine for days when you're on set and another routine for days when you're not on set. Have those in place so you don't just throw your routine away completely every time you get a job. You may have an A-Day, where you have plenty of free time to do all the things you want and need to do. But have a B-Day, too, when you can only do half those things. Finally, it's okay to have a C-Day, when only the most critical tasks will be completed. Give yourself permission to move between those routines and not feel guilty about it, but hold yourself accountable to them.

I had a client who shared parenting responsibilities with her ex-husband. She couldn't always stick to her schedule because, when she had her kids, she wanted to spend all her time with them. Exercise, meditation, and healthy eating habits went out the window on those days. She gave up on all her healthy practices on the days she had the kids and felt guilty about it later.

Actors have days like that. There are some days when our schedules are so full, it's tough to meditate or get to the gym. I worked with my client to develop a plan for her A-Days (kid*less* days), and one for her B-Days (kid*ful* days) when her healthy plans weren't going to happen. For her, A-Days include working out for an hour, meditating fifteen minutes twice a day, and cooking lunch and dinner at home. On her B-Days, she would do fifteen minutes of meditation in the morning, do some kind of active movement with the kids at some point during the day, and eat one healthy meal at home. That was a workable plan for her life and her priorities.

Your B-Day plan doesn't give you free reign to ditch all of your progress. It's a plan that takes less time, is less restrictive, and fits around the challenges of your schedule. Having a B-Day can remove the guilt of not following every rule you've imposed on yourself. It will keep you from falling completely off the wagon so you can get back to your regular routine quickly. It takes your life into consideration and helps set you up to win.

Actors can benefit from an A-Day for non-rehearsal or off-set days and a B-Day for rehearsal or on-set days. When I'm in rehearsal until 11 o'clock at night, I still have to get up with my kids in the morning—there's no way I'll get enough sleep. I schedule a nap on those days, which means something else isn't going to happen. I might have to skip yoga class and settle for ten minutes of stretching—that's my B-Day.

Most of us have several repeating patterns in our lives: days when we have the kids or don't have the kids, are in a show or aren't in a show, are working our day job or aren't working our day job. It's easy to get frazzled and give up completely on your schedule and healthy habits on those days. That's why having a B-Day, and even a C-Day and a D-Day, are so important. They allow you alternatives to your best possible days so you don't lose all that great momentum you've built up with your healthy lifestyle. It's another example of anticipating and preparing for probable obstacles.

TIME SAVERS

You can't create more hours in the day, but you can be more efficient with how you spend your time. You probably have tasks that could be automated. You might be doing tasks that someone else could be doing. Being aware of *how* you spend time will allow you to free up hours in the day.

Do you pay your bills with checks? The usual process is to first get the bills in the mail, open the envelopes, find a pen, your checkbook, and stamps (if you remembered to buy them). Then you fill out the payment forms, the checks, the envelopes, and your checkbook register. Finally, you have to get them to the mailbox or the post office. How much time could you save each month with automatic payments set up through your bank, a credit card, or Venmo?

Do you do things for your partner that they could be doing? Show them how to do those tasks, errands, and chores. Don't complain if they don't do them just like you would; offloading the tasks is giving you more time to do more important tasks.

If you have to run several errands in the week, batch them together and schedule an hour or two to knock them all out in one trip.

Call on your friends for help. We aren't all busy at the same time, so don't be afraid to ask a friend to help you out with an errand, and then be sure to reciprocate. You can pick up their dry cleaning or feed their dog when they have a late rehearsal, and they can do the same for you. Sometimes we have to lean on each other to get through this acting life sanely and without sacrificing our health and happiness.

Buying and preparing food can take time out of your day. In most cities, you can order groceries online and have them delivered, which could save you hours every week.

Amazon has a Subscribe & Save program, with discounts on automatic deliveries of products like cases of toilet paper or granola bars. Costco, Whole Foods, and other stores have online food delivery service through Instacart, in some cities, and sites like Thrive Market offer discounted, shelf-stable healthy food delivery. You can have restaurant meals delivered to your home with dozens of apps, or have ingredients and recipes for meals you cook yourself delivered from subscription services like Green Chef, Blue Apron, and Sun Basket.

Cooking several meals at a time is more efficient than cooking each one separately. Take a couple of hours on the weekend to cook up a weeks' worth of food. Make several different meals at once and freeze them for later, or cook up a family-size meal and freeze the extra servings. Chop up vegetables and have them handy in baggies in the fridge for quick, grab-and-go, nutrient-rich snacks. You'll be less likely to waste your time in line at the coffee shop for that expensive, high-carb, sugar-packed muffin.

If you know it's going to be a hectic couple of weeks, anticipate potential problems and have solutions ready. Get what you need together in your audition kit so you can grab everything—a script, a book, a healthy snack—on the way out the door. Plan to spend your downtime productively.

Look for other ways to find extra time. Are you spending

time on group activities that aren't interesting or useful to you? Don't be afraid to quit. Your time is a limited resource and you can give it away or use it to your best advantage.

Re-evaluate your workout routines. You don't need to spend an hour and a half at the gym every day. High-intensity interval training can give you a great workout in twenty minutes, three times a week. Look for ways to be more efficient with your workouts, and any other routines you've grown accustomed to over the years. Do they still make sense? If they don't, change them. You may be able to get the same results in much less time. Walk or bike your errands to increase movement and outdoor time.

TIME WASTERS

Pay attention to where your time goes. It's easy to tell yourself that you're "just going to check Facebook/Pinterest/Twitter" and then get sucked into social media quicksand. Three hours later, you emerge from reading all the updates on your sites and you have nothing to show for that time. Identify the pitfalls and set boundaries for yourself. Avoid the typical time wasters—television, social media, and internet—until after the important tasks are done. Set a time limit on each of them and set an alarm or a timer that reminds you your time is up. Apps like RescueTime and Freedom track your online time with tools to help you manage it.

MAXIMIZE YOUR NATURAL ENERGY

We all have natural rhythms and times of day when we're more productive. When do you get your best work done? When do you slow down? Are you a morning person, or are you a night owl who gets a surge of energy in the evening hours? Identify your high-energy and low-energy periods and tweak your daily schedule accordingly.

Some tasks require mental energy and focus, while you can almost sleepwalk through others. I have to be totally present when I work with clients, so I see them during my most productive times. I don't waste that time folding laundry. Likewise, I don't watch television during the day because that would be a waste of high-energy time that I could devote to more challenging activities.

Identify your most energetic times and plan to do your hardest work during those times. If you use your most productive time for the most difficult tasks, you'll do a better job and finish them more quickly. Schedule easy tasks for times when you're at your lowest points of the day.

Take some time to figure this out. At the end of the day, write down when you felt the most energetic and when you struggled. Maybe you should move some things around. Try it and then note the results. Michael Breus' book, *The Power of When*, is a guide for determining your body's chronotype beyond "night owl" and "early bird," so you can schedule everything you do at the best times for you. See how productive you can be by taking advantage of your high-energy times of the day.

MOTIVATE YOURSELF

A plan is terrific—if you follow it. How do you stay motivated enough to follow your own schedule?

Look at your schedule every day. You can look it over at night or first thing in the morning. It's easier to be motivated and productive when you have a nicely laid out schedule to follow that's going to give you what you want.

If you have a huge task, break it into bite-sized pieces. You may not be able to learn all your lines in one day, but you *can* learn scenes one and two, for example. You *can* clean one room in your house or organize one drawer. Be honest with yourself about what's possible, and if your list is manageable you'll be more likely to tackle it.

Start with your goals. What can you do to advance your goals? If one of your goals is to lose ten pounds, what can you do to get closer to that goal? You might do a strength training routine, go to a cardio class, or do a dozen kettlebell swings several times throughout the day. Pick something you'll have time to do.

While you're looking over your goals, remind yourself of why you set them in the first place. Why do you want to lose ten pounds? Why do you want to clean your house? What are you getting out of it? Maybe your clothes will fit better if you're a little lighter, and maybe you'll feel calmer and less stressed if your apartment is neat. Think about how you'll feel when those things are done so you're motivated to take steps to make them happen.

Every evening, I write a short list of what I want to get done the next day. If you're planning your schedule every week, this should be an easy task. There's a tendency to get too ambitious and overcrowd the list, so it helps to write down everything I want to accomplish and then pick the most important tasks. Pick three to five tasks that will make the greatest impact toward achieving your goals. What's the most important goal that will contribute to your success? Start with that one. If you choose too many, then you may not accomplish any of them.

Start the day off right by accomplishing a difficult task first thing in the morning. Don't waste that time watching the morning news or reading the latest Facebook updates; do that one important task that you've probably been putting off. Prioritize your tasks and get the most important one done right away, when you have the most energy and willpower. You'll get some momentum from your accomplishment. Then you can keep going and tackle the next task. If something or someone throws a wrench into your schedule and interrupts your momentum, you at least got the most important thing done and you'll be closer to your goals and have a tremendous sense of accomplishment.

Some people aren't naturally self-disciplined, but, with practice, you can develop a habit of following daily routines that get you closer to your goals. Motivate yourself to work out, practice your lines, go to that audition, and meditate. Remind yourself why you're doing all this. Nothing happens until you do it and self-motivation is the only way you'll do what you need to do to reach your goals and satisfy all your *whys*. Regardless of which plan or goal you choose, really do it. As Maya Angelou put it, "Nothing will work unless you do."

If you have a task that's tough to focus on for a long period of time, try the Pomodoro Technique—the time management method where you complete twenty-five minutes of an activity at a time, separated by short breaks. If you have a task that takes fifty minutes to complete, work on it for twenty-five minutes, take a five, then go for another twenty-five minutes.

Developing good habits and decreasing the bad ones are important steps to achieving the goals you set, so motivate yourself to stick to your daily habits. New technologies can provide positive reinforcement that helps you develop good habits. A habit tracker app for your phone or computer will help you track habits, and you can set reminders and even set up competitions with friends who are also trying to develop good habits. Some apps use negative reinforcement to train you to stop participating in habits that keep you from reaching your goals; for example, one has a feature that makes you donate to a charity you wouldn't typically support if you don't complete your daily habits!

Relying on willpower might work for some people, but most of us have to write down our intentions. *The Resilient Actor's Workbook* will help you create a plan. Start right now by scheduling a few tasks in your phone, on your computer, or on a paper calendar on the wall. If you put them in writing and assign a time for them, you'll be more likely to do them.

WHAT CAN I DO TODAY?

An organized plan will put you on the path toward productivity. Decluttering your space and schedule clears the path. Simply being aware of your most and least productive times allows you to make better decisions about how you spend your day. Take a few moments to think through the following exercises and jot down your thoughts on each. Then take twenty more minutes to tackle one. Hang onto those notes and you can tackle the other exercises later today or this week.

- Look around you: Is the room neat or cluttered? What about the rest of your home? Could you be featured on a show about hoarders? Pledge to declutter one area of your home today. Clean up one pile of clothes, go through one stack of papers, or donate one box of items to Goodwill. Write down your first declutter target and what you're going to do about it.

- What are your time wasters? Do you have a social media or TV habit? Write down how much time you spent on each of your time wasters today. If you don't know for sure, give yourself a rough estimate. Now keep a running tab for the rest of the day. Pledge to split that time in half tomorrow. What will you accomplish with that extra time? Write it down. Treat screen time like dessert.

- When is your most productive time? Do you get most of your work done first thing in the morning, mid-morning, or late at night? Now choose your toughest task—the one you keep putting off. Schedule that task during your next period of high energy and productivity. If you have a job outside of acting and your high energy time falls during work hours, figure out a next-best time. When do you really buckle down and get things done? Make that tough task your #1 task when your high productivity time rolls around. Write down the time and task now—and commit to doing it.

PRACTICE(S) MAKES PROGRESS

Your goals may seem like a distant dream. Can you really have the life you imagined? Can you live where you want to live, do the kind of work you want to do, and be the kind of person you want to be? You can—and you don't need a fairy godmother or even a magic wand to get there. You just need practices—regular habits and regular actions that move you closer to your goals.

Define practices that move you closer to your acting goals, your health goals, and all your other goals. Schedule your practices on a calendar and track your progress in a journal, daily planner, or workbook. If you do a little bit each day you'll make steady daily, weekly, and monthly progress. It adds up!

The calendar fairies aren't going to show up to do this for you. You have to figure out your *whys*, set your goals, and decide which practices work for you. You have to schedule them, motivate yourself to do them, and track your progress. It may sound complicated, but it isn't; it's your life, so it's worth putting in the time and effort.

What questions can you ask yourself to help develop your goals? What practices should you do to meet them? How do you stay on track and make steady progress?

The Resilient Actor's Workbook includes many of the questions I ask my clients and a plan for tracking weekly and daily practices. Below is a sampling of tasks you can incorporate into your own plan. Design your plan to reach your goals and move you closer to the life you imagined, visualized, and wrote about in the first chapter of this book.

You can live your ideal life. It starts right here, right now.

CRAFT PRACTICES

You have to find a home base. Whether it be a small theater company you do readings with, or a weekly workshop, an acting class, a voice lesson, a bar. You'll go crazy if the only place you're practicing your craft is at auditions.

—DAVE THOMAS BROWN, *AMERICAN PSYCHO*, BROADWAY; *THE LEGEND OF GEORGIA MCBRIDE*, *HEATHERS*, OFF-BROADWAY; *BRIDGES OF MADISON COUNTY*, FIRST NATIONAL TOUR

Actors don't go to acting school, become actors, and then quit developing or refining their craft. They continually hone their skills. You've heard the quote from Roman philosopher Seneca, "Luck is what happens when preparation meets opportunity." That's exactly *why* you have to practice your craft. If you aren't prepared when an opportunity arises, you won't be that "lucky" actor who gets the part.

Always be honing your skills to stay in top form, and not just when you're in a film or show. Between shows, prepare for your next audition. If you don't have an audition lined up, prepare anyway. You never know when a casting will come up, but you'll always be ready if you take time every week to work on your skills.

Pick out material for auditioning and memorize songs and monologues. Take acting classes and workshops. Do stage readings to keep your chops up. If you're a vocalist, practice your scales, do your vocal workout, and hire a vocal coach if you can afford one to help you continually improve your voice.

Start a play or screenplay reading group. Get some actor friends together, pick a play or film, and meet weekly to read together. It's great for your cold reading skills, and if you have the event scheduled with other people you're more likely to do it. Reading with other people is more fun than sitting alone in your apartment reading by yourself.

Ask yourself, "What are the daily practices I need to do to keep my skills up? What can I do weekly?" Write them down and, when you plan your week, be sure to fit them into your schedule. If you don't put them on a calendar, they won't get done. If you schedule them—and practice— you might get "lucky." You will get hired.

BUSINESS PRACTICES

Practicing your craft will keep your skills up so you can get hired after an audition. You also need to schedule regular business practices so you *have* opportunities to audition.

Check in with your agent regularly. Don't wait around for her to call you. Set a regular time to call her and see if she has any work for you, or if there's anything she needs from you to help her get you more work. If you have a talent manager, check in with him too. Ask them how often they want you to check in.

Don't depend on your agent to keep you employed. Attend open auditions. Schedule time every week to check the breakdowns. Read the trades. Fish around online and see what's coming up and what you can audition for right now. Check all the theater and production company websites to see what's out there. This is the job part of the job, remember? That perfect role isn't going to fall into your lap.

Make it a point to sit down once a month or every season and write up a list of all the shows that are coming up. Narrow the list to those that are a good fit, and then get the material you need to prepare for those auditions. The earlier you start, the more prepared you'll be, and the better you'll do at the audition. Log who you contacted, who you auditioned for and any feedback you received.

BUILD YOUR BRAND

These days, it's essential to have a professional online presence whether it's via Instagram, Twitter, Facebook, or your own website.

—ALLISON SPRATT PEARCE, *CURTAINS*, *CRY BABY*, *GOOD VIBRATIONS*, BROADWAY; WWW.ALLISONSPRATTPEARCE.COM

Take time to market yourself. Send out your headshots and resume to the casting directors listed on the breakdowns. Update your resume after every job and print out a few copies so you aren't scrambling to rewrite the whole thing when you need it.

Set up a website and maintain it. Design your site to reflect your best you and those characteristics that make you unique. If you're chili, your website should represent chili. If you have time, you can add a blog, but be sure to keep it positive. You can be human and vulnerable too. Remember, nobody expects you to be perfct (see what I did there?). Humor is a good quality to show off in your blog.

Always keep your posts professional. You never know who's looking, and your posts may be seen by producers, directors, and other people with casting authority. If they click on your page and see a bunch of political tirades and cat videos, what are they going to think of you? Your internet presence can have a real effect on your career, so think about what you're putting out there. Don't ever post anything you wouldn't want your favorite director to see. That stuff can linger out there forever; and, even if it doesn't hurt your career right away, it may come back to haunt you down the road.

You can add a downloadable resume and links to your social media sites. Be sure to have contact information on your site. A contact page, email address, or phone number make it easy for directors to reach out to you about your work and availability.

Be yourself with your internet presence. Once you know who you really are, that's the person you need to be showing the world. People will get to know and like that best version of you, so you need to keep reminding them why they fell in love with you in the first place. If you go off on tangents—especially negative tangents—people may feel confused and misled, or they may be offended or lose interest in you. Figure out who you are and then stay true to your best self.

STRENGTHEN YOUR NETWORK

In this day and age, actors have to maintain an active social media presence. Use social media to touch base with the acting community. Post career updates to let people know when you're doing a reading or showcase, or when your project airs.

Send thank you notes to people who help you out. A hand-written note can go a long way toward helping someone remember you. Some people send out or email reviews and clippings to let people know they're working. You have to continually market yourself—nicely. You can let people know what you're up to without stalking them or being obnoxious about it. Keep your notes short, sweet, sincere, and relevant.

Ask people in the industry what *they're* doing. People love to talk about themselves, especially to other people who are genuinely interested in them. Listen to what they have to say.

LOOK SHARP

Maintaining your appearance is part of any serious actor's

routine. This isn't about vanity—it's part of the job. Keep yourself in good physical shape, keep your hair cut and colored to match your headshots, and keep your nails trimmed or manicured. Take care of your teeth and get them whitened if they need it. You needn't look like a soap opera actor (unless you actually *are* a soap opera actor), but you should always look neat and well maintained whenever you go out in public.

If you need some serious work done, like a nose job or other plastic surgery, that's your choice. It isn't the right way to go for everyone, but if it's the best choice for you then more power to you. Do your research and go to somebody reputable. A bad surgical procedure can really mess up your health and your appearance.

SEE—AND BE SEEN

See theater. See as much as you can afford.

—DAVE THOMAS BROWN, *AMERICAN PSYCHO*, BROADWAY; *THE LEGEND OF GEORGIA MCBRIDE*, *HEATHERS*, OFF-BROADWAY; *BRIDGES OF MADISON COUNTY*, FIRST NATIONAL TOUR

It's easy to stay home and make excuses for why you don't want to go out—but you'll never regret showing up to support actors and other people in the business. Go to the theater and see other people's shows. Go to the movies and see other people's films. Seeing other people's work is an opportunity to learn more about acting. You can't grow as an actor if you're in a vacuum.

Take a shower, dress up, put on some lipstick, and get out there and enjoy yourself. Be happy and positive and be open to talking to everybody. They'll be happy to see you, and you'll be glad you got out there and showed everyone you're still around. If you show up to support their work, maybe they'll show up sometime to support yours.

Think about producing your own material. Write a one-man show. Is there a role you've always wanted to play but no one ever cast you in? Write the role, put your own spin on it, and cast yourself in it. Talk to theater owners or producers and see if there's an off-night where you can present your show. It's a lot of work to do your own show, but if you get it out there you can record it and then post your video online to promote yourself.

Look for other opportunities to get in front of an audience. Make mini-movies and publish them on YouTube. If you have a stand-up routine, check out the open mic nights at local comedy clubs. Look for open cabaret nights to sing, and storytelling nights at coffee shops. It's great experience for you, and you never know who's going to be there!

Use those performances as an opportunity to build relationships. Chat with people before and after the show.

You don't have to be annoying about it, but if people enjoy your performance, they'll want to know more about you. They may want to hire you.

Get creative with your business practices. Ask yourself, "What could I be doing to advance my career?" Brainstorm some new ideas and look for time slots on your schedule to squeeze them in.

This might all sound overwhelming, but if you do a little bit every week, you'll make progress, inch by inch.

MIND PRACTICES

Develop a morning routine that puts you in a calm, positive mood. Some practices that set the tone for a calmer mindset and prepare you for a more productive day (even if you don't get out of bed until noon) include: yoga, meditation, stretching, a few interval sets or bodyweight exercises, inspirational reading, journaling, or affirmations. Experiment with different methods to find the best combination of morning rituals. The book *The Miracle Morning* by Hal Elrod goes into great detail about morning routines, so if you need help creating one that suits you, check out his book. The theory is, if you do a concentrated routine of self-care—a string of healthy habits in the morning— you've already gotten a lot accomplished and are setting yourself up to win.

Add mini-routines throughout the day to calm your mind. You might start your morning with three minutes of breathing exercises, then do fifteen minutes of tai chi after lunch, and add thirty minutes of yoga twice a week. Pick your best times for power poses, affirmations, tapping, and other mind practices that work for you. Schedule them and take breaks for them to keep you in the right frame of mind throughout the day.

Daily and weekly periods of meditation, breathing, or mindfulness that calm your nerves and encourage you to be present will give you the peace and balance in your life that you need to offset the unpredictability of your acting schedule.

Make time to journal every day. Journaling is like having a free therapist who's always there for you. Taking just a few minutes to write in your planner or journal lets you release the monkeys off the repetitive treadmill—those useless thoughts that replay over and over in your head, wasting your time and bringing you down. Dump all your stray thoughts into a journal and then focus on the important tasks you have to tackle that day. Journaling is a great late-night activity to get all those thoughts out of your head before you go to sleep. Julia Cameron's *The Artist's Way* suggests three unedited "morning pages" to clean out your brain every morning.

Cook up your own combination of activities for maintaining a calm, happy brain. If you choose activities you enjoy and schedule them at times of day when you're more inclined to do them, you'll have a higher chance of success.

If serious issues are popping up for you, practices alone may not be enough. Seek professional help and deal with them. Don't let all that baggage fester and hold you back—clean it up. A good therapist can help you clean up any emotional junk or trauma lingering from your past. If you can't afford to hire someone, check into services that the Actor's Fund provides, and see if your insurance has any coverage you can take advantage of to get the help you need.

There are 12-step programs and support groups out there for just about everything, so don't go it alone. It's your life and you create everything in it, so take full responsibility and seek out the healthiest habits and resources to build your reserves.

BODY PRACTICES

Practices for your body include self-care tasks and activities to improve and maintain your physical health.

Commit to buying high-quality, organic ingredients at

the grocery store, preparing nutrient-rich, healthy meals at home (when you can), and making good choices when you eat out.

Schedule time on your calendar for grocery shopping and cooking so you're not tempted to buy fast food. Leave time for food prep before you leave the house so you can pack a lunch and snacks to take with you. Planning ahead is especially important for days when you know you'll be rushing between errands or activities, or away from home for a while, like at an all-day audition. If you don't plan ahead, you might be tempted to settle for junk food or other unhealthy choices. Have a few default healthy meals at some of your regular restaurants on your route. I know that I can always get a grass-fed burger on a vegetable salad to go at Burger Lounge. It's my go-to fast meal on the run.

Incorporate movement breaks into your daily schedule. You don't have to do weights, cardio, and stretching every day, but you should be doing *something* daily. If you're in a dance production or taking dance classes, that counts as exercise. Cross-train with a variety of exercise routines throughout the week to reduce the chances of overuse and injury. Don't get into a boring exercise rut with just one activity—mix it up.

If you don't have twenty minutes to spare, take two-minute

exercise breaks. Get some hand weights or kettlebells and do ten-rep sets of one or two exercises every hour—like squats, curls, or push-ups—so you get a full workout and stay energized throughout the day. Short, hourly workouts also help you avoid sitting in one place for many hours at a time, which is incredibly unhealthy! Do ten squats while the coffee is brewing or the computer printer is printing. Put the weights in an obvious place like your bathroom, kitchen, or by the television, so you can grab them and squeeze in those reps. Make them visible so you remember to use them. If they're hidden away in a closet, you'll forget about them.

You may not actually calendar your sleep time, but make sure you get *enough* of it to fully recover. If you're an eight-hour person, plan to get eight hours of sleep every night, even if that means coming straight home after a show. Schedule naps to make up for sleep shortages. Attempt to maintain a consistent sleep schedule as best you can. Getting enough sleep may not seem like a big deal, but it's one of the most overlooked and challenging disciplines to develop. The daily and long-term payoffs of a regular sleep schedule are tremendous, so be nice to your body and give it the rest it needs. Schedule your sleep and don't skimp on it.

PRACTICES THAT MAKE THE BIGGEST IMPACT

What actions could have the greatest impact on your career? Figure out what you need to do every day and every week to get your acting game on and schedule it. Make it happen for yourself.

If you've been following along with me and taking notes, you probably have a list of practices to follow for your craft, the business of acting, and your mind and body. You can't do everything every day, but the goal is to do *something* in each category every week.

Look at your lists and start prioritizing. What can you do that'll have the biggest impact on your happiness and your acting career? Be honest with yourself, and don't start with the easiest task to give you that quick dopamine hit from checking a checkbox. Really think about the best choices that'll move you closer to your goals. Read each item and think about the outcome of making each one of them a daily or weekly practice.

Choose a practice from each category that'll have the greatest impact. Knowing your weaknesses will help you make that decision. What are your weaknesses? Where do you need the most help right now? Where are you really slacking off? If you're in terrific shape, it'll be tempting to focus on diet and exercise, but maybe you should devote some serious time to your mindset, or the business side of your career. Be realistic about where you fall short. Only you can make the right decision, and only you can move your life closer to where you want it to be. Schedule your hardest, most impactful practices during your highest energy and willpower times and you'll be more willing to do them, and do them well.

Go back to your SMART goals. Read them and remind yourself of why you set them in the first place. Think about your *why*. That'll help you choose impactful practices and will also motivate you to follow through with them. What are the daily actions, the big little steps that will move you in the right direction?

Schedule your practices. You can schedule each one for the same time every day, or you may have to move them around to whatever times you have available outside of work and other responsibilities. Do your best to include at least one for your mind, body, craft, and career every day. You can also have weekly practices, and some practices that only make sense to do once a month. If you complete just one practice in each category every week, you'll make progress!

Plan for success. Set yourself up to win. If your yoga class is on the other side of town and you're battling traffic both ways, you won't look forward to going to class and you won't come home relaxed and rejuvenated—so what's the point? If that's the case, find another location for that class or pick another activity that works for you.

Some activities can serve many purposes. For example, hiking a few miles on a trail is a great cardiovascular exercise for your body. It may also keep you at your ideal weight, give you some nature time, and clear your head. A good hike may help you sleep better at night.

Develop routines that you can plug in throughout the day and the week and monitor the results. If something is working—fantastic. Keep that practice on your schedule. If something isn't working, dump it, tweak it, or do less of it. There's more than one way to get where you're going, and everyone's path is different. Make your own path, follow it, track your progress, and make adjustments as needed. Don't be afraid to evolve.

CUT YOURSELF SOME SLACK

There will be times when you're working hard and you'll have to focus on just getting enough sleep. That might mean cutting a workout short, so give yourself permission to do that. Sometimes we get down to taking care of just the basic survival needs. Be in charge and do what's best for you, but don't be too hard on yourself, either. You can't do everything every day and if you try you'll just burn out—but don't confuse "burned out" with "lazy," either.

Leave room for downtime. Schedules are terrific and they'll get you where you want to go, but life is unpredictable and can be complicated. Unexpected events will arise, along with the usual day-to-day activities, so allow time in your schedule for tasks that have nothing to do with being a happy, healthy, resilient actor—like paying bills and calling the plumber. *Balance.*

Some practices are easier with an accountability buddy. If you need extra motivation, get someone to support you in reaching your goals. Ask your actor friends if they need to get new headshots or update their resumes, and then schedule a time to do it together. You don't have to do all your practices alone, and you might enjoy them more with friends around.

Gather the daily and weekly practices that will have the greatest impact on your life and your career, and plug them into your calendar. Having a schedule will improve your chances of doing what you need to do, and you can enjoy a sense of accomplishment every time you complete a new task. You'll reap the rewards of health, happiness, and resilience as you move forward toward your goals.

CONSIDER A PERSONAL COACH

Similar to finding a therapist, working with a good coach depends on trust and personality. Don't be afraid to try a few

until you find one you like. And then stick with them. Many
actors stop coaching just around the time things get challeng-
ing—this is the time that the work starts getting really good!

—ERIN CRONICAN, THE ACTORS' ENTERPRISE

What good is a coach? Do you need one? I'm biased when
it comes to personal coaches because I've received a lot of
help from coaching and had great results. I'm also a certified
coach, so I've seen what coaching has done for my clients.

Some of the most successful people in the world—movers,
shakers, athletes, performers, entrepreneurs, bazillion-
aires, and people who want to excel in any field—have
coaches that help them reach their goals.

Shop around and find a coach you trust. Not all coaches
are created equal. A good coach goes through extensive
training and stays current in her education. She's a great
listener and she's objective. While your friends and family
may also be great listeners, a coach is outside your close
circle of family and friends, so you can share your thoughts
and feelings with her and not have to worry about your
words being shared with other people in your circle. A
good coach takes your privacy seriously, so whatever you
tell her is confidential—assuming you aren't discussing
doing bodily harm to yourself or others.

A coach will be honest with you and won't just tell you

what you *want* to hear, but what you *need* to hear—that's her job. If you don't succeed, your coach doesn't succeed. Think about it this way: you're hiring someone to help you become your best you. If you can afford a personal coach, why wouldn't you get one?

A personal coach will work with you one-on-one in person, by phone, or through video conferencing. You can meet with your coach every month, every week, or as often as you like. A good coach will ask questions to discover your current situation, help you determine what you want your life to look like, and then help you get there.

Coaches can focus on specific aspects of your life and career. They can also hold you accountable, which can motivate you to stay on track long enough to develop new, good habits. She'll focus on you and your goals, and give you honest feedback. A good coach customizes the sessions to your needs and goals and helps you on a path to self-discovery, action, and accountability. She'll be in your corner and want you to succeed.

Your coach should be able to match your pace. She may challenge you, but she shouldn't pressure you to do things you're not prepared to do, or simply don't want to do. A coaching relationship, although challenging, should be positive so you'll look forward to your sessions together.

Coaching is individualized. You can read self-help books and websites, but it can be daunting to figure out how any of it applies to you. It can also be overwhelming to figure out what's most important to you as an individual, or how you're going to fit it all in. A coach will help you figure that out and motivate you to follow through with your plans.

Be selective when choosing a coach. Depending on his or her specialty, they should be certified by a governing body, such as the International Coach Federation (ICF) or the Association of Coaches (AC). They should have proper training with a reputable program and be able to provide you with references.

Request an introductory consult or a complimentary session with a coach, or try out a coach for a few sessions and decide if coaching is a good fit for you. If they're really helping you move forward, then stick with them. You may actually only need a few sessions to get on track. Some people retain coaches for years, while others just need a coach to get them through a rough patch. Ideally, you'll work with your coach for at least three to six months so they can get to know you better and provide you with greater long-term benefits. It's hard to change your life without some consistent effort and feedback.

A coach can help you get to the next level with your health, happiness, and career, but a coach is not a therapist. If you have serious, debilitating emotional challenges, trauma, or problems with addiction, get medical help specific to your needs.

A coach will help to lay the groundwork and motivate you, but in the end, you need to do what needs to be done. I've seen remarkable results from people who benefited from coaching. Just having the guidance, support, and accountability can make a huge difference in your life.

Consider getting a personal coach to accelerate your progress toward reaching your life and career goals.

At 70, I worked with a life coach for the first time! Trusting someone else with your real self can be an amazing eye-opener. The barrier is, you have to TRUST.

—SUE B., ACTOR/SINGER AND COACHING CLIENT

WHAT CAN I DO TODAY?

Practices are where you put actions to your ideas. What practices will you adopt this week, and how will they change your life? There's only one way to find out. Start with the following activities and make them regular practices. It's go time.

- How would you like to start your day? What habits can you fit into thirty to sixty minutes to really put you on track for the day? Develop a morning routine and commit to starting it tomorrow. Write it down and put it on your bathroom mirror so you'll see it first thing in the morning. Tweak it each day until you settle on the perfect morning routine.

- What one practice will have the greatest impact on your career? What practices will have the greatest impact on honing your craft and improving your mental and physical health? Choose one practice in each category. They can be daily or weekly practices. Write them down and schedule them on your calendar. Completing one practice will give you a great sense of accomplishment and the momentum you need to keep going. Then celebrate! Do your happy dance, call your best friend and tell her what you did. Pat yourself on the back—you deserve it.

- Is there something you need a little extra help with? Are you stuck with your exercise routine, your personal relationships, or stuck in your career? Go online and find a coach who provides the support you need. Call them and ask for an introductory trial session.

SCENE 9

FINALE

You want to stay sane and develop resilience as an actor, right? Well, I've laid out a lot of tools, tricks, hacks and ideas for you—so many that you may feel overwhelmed! That's not the goal here—the goal is to kick ass in the business without letting the business kick your ass, so you can enjoy a happy, healthy life and career. So where to start?

You can't do everything in this book all at once, and you may *never* be able to do it all. Pick the ideas that resonate with you and solve a problem that you've been avoiding. Start a new habit you've been putting off.

I recommend starting with your health. Without it, you can't do the rest. Your health is precious. Although I've offered you plenty of advice for improving your health, ultimately, it's up to you to make healthy choices. No coach, trainer, or book can do that for you. You've got to make your own choices *every day,* with *every meal.* You choose what to eat, when to go to bed, and whether to exercise. You choose to meditate or watch TV. You choose positive thoughts over that negative monologue that keeps replaying in your head. You choose to call a friend and make that contact or sit alone in your apartment. You make those choices and no one else can make them for you. You have that responsibility, but you also have that control.

Every choice you make and action you take has consequences, positive or negative. You control those consequences with your choices, and your decisions add up—with compounding interest!

Develop goals and an action plan to accomplish them. Time is limited and if you don't manage it to get what you want, time will slip away from you and your progress will be limited. Make an honest assessment of where you are and where you want to be. Look at your strengths and weaknesses. Capitalize on them, or do something about them.

Cultivate your best self, for you and for your audience. The actor's life is a balancing act and we all go through easy times and hard times, feasts and famines. The more organized and prepared we are, and the more balanced our lives are, the easier it'll be to take advantage of opportunities and survive the pitfalls.

I know actors who are struggling, unhealthy, and tired. I also know actors who are thriving, healthy, and loving life. It's up to you to choose that good life and go after it. Every moment won't be filled with happy, positive thinking, and it's healthy to feel all the emotional colors. Judging yourself and beating yourself up for feeling negative emotions is counterproductive. We're designed to feel anger, sadness, and jealousy; so accept and deal with those feelings, but don't allow them to hold you back or keep you from reaching your goals. You aren't doing anything wrong if you occasionally feel sad, angry, lazy, or stressed. Accept those feelings and keep going.

Acting can be exhilarating and rewarding. Relish the creativity, the play, the laughter, and the camaraderie of it. Enjoy the silliness, and breathe. Do the work but don't take it so seriously that you forget why you became an actor.

Remember earlier in this book when you were visualizing your perfect life? Think about that for a moment. Really imagine how it would feel to be in that life. If you start working toward that life right now, where will you be in three months? If you continue on the same path you're on now and make no changes at all, what'll your life look like in three months? Which life do you choose—and why wait?

LIGHTS, CAMERA, ACTION!

We're near the end and I give you tremendous credit for reading the whole book. Yay! Many people don't have the discipline or desire to create a better life for themselves. You've taken a major first step: wanting a better life and career and doing something about it. Now take action. Don't just put this book down and turn on the television or head to the refrigerator. Reading a book isn't enough. Act right now and set your life in a new direction, the direction of health, happiness, and reaching your goals.

Where to start?

Pick three things.

Right now.

Get out the companion guide to this book, *The Resilient Actor's Workbook*, or a notebook, or even a scrap of paper. Write down three actions that'll move you forward. Your three tasks may not be earth-shattering and can be as simple as bringing your lunch to rehearsal instead of eating less healthy food, taking a weekly yoga class, or doing five minutes of meditation every day. It's okay to start small, but one of your three tasks might be a major and potentially life-changing decision or activity—like getting an agent to help you with your career, or getting a day job that's less stressful than the one you have now.

If you do something positive right now—right this minute—you'll get some momentum. Do a push-up. One push-up. Program one healthy reminder into your phone. Call a friend and see if she wants to join you for a run in the park. You can tell her about all the changes you have planned for your life, how excited you are to get started, and how amazing the coming days, months, and year will be. You'll have more energy, and once you start, you'll want to keep going. Remember that consistency matters.

Let me know how you're doing. You can contact me anytime at www.DebraWanger.com and tell me about your struggles and your successes. I'd love to hear about what you've learned and what I can learn from you. We're all in this together. No matter what's happened in the past, no matter where you were or where you are right now, the rest of it is in your hands and you have the power to make it your best life, starring the best version of you. This is your movie. You're the writer, the director, and the star!

I look forward to seeing you on stage, on television, or in a movie. I look forward to working with you some day. And I wish you luck, grace, and joy.

Go forth and kick ass.

ACKNOWLEDGMENTS

I want to acknowledge a slew of people for helping me learn and grow as a human, actor, mother, coach, and author, and for getting me to where I am now. These people helped directly and indirectly in creating and shaping this book: Calvin, Madelyn and Gwen, Phoebe Telser, Ralph Wanger, Leah Zell, Gene Telser, Eric Wanger, Len Wanger, Elise Wanger, Jenny Wanger, Kat, Zach, Becca, Max, Ian and Ivy, Dave Asprey, Dr. Mark Atkinson, Rod Francis, Ronit LeMon Drobey, Lane Kennedy, Cheryl Bayer, Josh Lieberman, Joan Hyler, Jeff Saver, Lori Hammel, Phil Johnson, Dr. Seth Krosner, Omri Schein, Joel Newsome, Sean Murray, Bill Schmidt, Edward Sayegh, Tom Stephenson, Steve Glaudini, Bets Malone, Seema Sueko, Sam Woodhouse, Paula Kalustian, Dr. Terry O'Donnell, Dr. Dude Stephenson, Dr. Rick Simas, Dr. Aubrey Berg, Kristi Holden, Allison Spratt Pearce, Spencer Moses, Allen Kendall, Dave Thomas Brown, Courtney Corey,

Erin Cronican, Sharon Donaldson-Wheatley, Pressley Sutherland, Rob Chafin, Beth Blankenship Thomson, Melissa Wheat Kelly, Paul Morgavo, E.Y. Washington, Bryan & Katie Banville, Melissa & Manny Fernandes, Linda Libby, Sarah Palmer Marion, Amy Perkins, Dr. Alex Nemiroski, Donny Gersonde, Michael Cusimano, Vanessa Dinning, Michael Mizerany, Adi Mullen, Kathie Ross, Amy Rogers, Jill Collister Gould, Lori Lum, Michael Tahaney, Jim Brown, Ashlee Espinosa, Randall Eames, Ryan Scrimger, Eric Moore, Nick Spear, Rebecca Spear, Cari Bell-Deduke, Robert Meffe, Peter Herman, Arno Selko, Linda Buzzell, Hal Elrod, Jon Berghoff, Juliana Reye, Jenna Bayne, Lindsay Coffman McCarthy, Victor Ramirez, John Negrete, Angie Buckingham Macdougall, Elizabeth Gilbert, John Gray, Halina Popko, Sarah Maes, Rita Berg, Nino Prodan, Kristen Strate, Daniel Bradley, David Christopher Lawson, Emily Baker, Thaddeus Owen, Chris James, Todd Shipman, Dr. Stan Shapiro, Dr. Amanda Ward, Joelle Neulander, Amy Russ, The Originals, my coaching clients, Jill and Robert J. Townsend, Erin and Gary Lewis, Linda Lee Beck, Claire Lane, Jean Fischer, Polly Nelson McClellan, John Fowler, Evelyn Terry, The Children's School, San Diego State University, Tufts University, the faculty of University of Cincinnati College-Conservatory of Music, the New Trier High School drama faculty and staff, Joyce & Byrne Piven, all of The Upgraded Women, The V.C.'s, The San Diego Bio-hackers Meetup, the San Diego theatre community, the

entire staff at Cygnet Theatre, San Diego Musical Theater
& Moonlight Amphitheatre, all my helpful & dear ones I
forgot and will probably remember as soon as this book
goes to print, and Zoey & Everest, the best dogs ever.

PHOTO: KEN JACQUES

ABOUT THE AUTHOR

Hailed as a "comic sparkplug" by the *Miami Herald*, **DEBRA WANGER** is an actor, author, and Certified Bulletproof Coach. She specializes in teaching actors how to balance a healthy lifestyle with an exciting, creative career.

Debra's performed in regional theaters and cabaret clubs across the country from Boston to Los Angeles, and her CD *Driving My Own Heart* is available on Amazon and iTunes.

As an assistant talent agent at Creative Artists Agency under super-agent Michael Ovitz, Debra helped guide the careers of top actors including Donald Sutherland, Patrick Dempsey, Halle Berry, Alyssa Milano, and Antonio Banderas.

She graduated magna cum laude from Tufts University with a BA in sociology and earned an MFA in musical theater, graduating Phi Kappa Phi from San Diego State University as a Marion Ross Scholar.

Debra is a member of the Association of Coaches. She co-hosts the *Upgraded Woman* podcast with Lane Kennedy, helping women upgrade themselves and live their best lives.

When she's not performing or coaching, Debra likes to play the guitar, harp, and piano, and explore creative adventures in cooking, aromatherapy, yoga, interior decorating, and chocolate. She lives in San Diego with her three children and their black lab, Zoey. You can contact Debra at her website www.DebraWanger.com.